# Love Must Mean Something

## A Sports Novel

By

Rick Birk

ISBN no. 978-0-9819964-1-7

Library of Congress categories: Sports. Sports Fiction. Sports events. Coaching. Ball Games.

**This book is easily available at go5books.com**

## What people are saying about
### *'Love Must Mean Something'*

"Birk, an Academy graduate, serves an ace with this exciting and inspiring tale of a young tennis player's struggles and triumphs, and her unwavering love for the game. *Love Must Mean Something* is truly motivating and fun. It will encourage generations of athletes to strive for their best, no matter what the competition, the obstacles or the outcome. Athletes and sports enthusiasts alike will enjoy this read and hopefully, as the character Nicole did, discover the competitor and dreamer that lies within."

*- United States Sports Academy*

"*Love Must Mean Something* glares into what the world of junior tennis can be like and hits a winner. A great read for junior players and their parents."

*- Jeff Sikes, Marketing and Communications Manager - USTA Southwest Section*

"The excitement, emotion and challenges of tennis and competition are cleverly captured by Rick Birk. This book reinforces the need to believe in yourself and proves that in life one must learn to adapt and play the ball regardless of the direction it bounces! Sport lovers of all ages will enjoy this book."

*- David C. Rogers - Tennis Professional, SportMinder Enterprises LLC*

"A wonderful story: Proof as to what dedication, determination and desire can do!"

*- Jeff Berman Athletic Director Boys and Girls Club of Greater Scottsdale*

"*Love Must Mean Something* by Rick Birk is an uplifting, inspiring book. It leaves you feeling that you can achieve anything through hard work, dedication, heart, and faith. Tennis players will be wrapped up in every exhilarating game Nicole plays because they will feel like they are actually in the rallies. The precise detail about strategy and technique make this book believable, accurate, and educational by truly getting into the mind of the athlete. Every page connects you to Nicole as you cheer her on point after point and through all of her obstacles and hardships. The lessons learned in this heartwarming story of a little girl competing in junior tennis tournaments can be applied to any sport or life goal, and is a must read for all athletes who need a little inspiration to keep pushing through to achieve their goals."

*- Caeli Barker - High School Tennis Player, Phoenix, Arizona*

# Dedication

My Dear Daughter Nicole,
Thank you for bringing so much fun and excitement into
my life. You are truly a gift from God.
                    Love,
                        Dad

# Acknowledgements

John Birk
Brad Cooper (Cooper Design Studios)
Sheila McInerney
Dr. Dennis Stadel
Mark Tichenor
Patrick Wood

# Tennis Anyone?

A game of tennis is generally played up to 4 points. These points are consecutively termed 15, 30, 40, and game. Having no points in a game is referred to having a score of 'love.' Each game must be won by a two point margin. If the game score is tied at 40-40 or any point thereafter, this is referred to as 'deuce.' If the server wins the next point, he is said to have the advantage or ad-in. If the non-server wins the point, he is said to have the advantage and this is referred to as ad-out. The score of the server is always announced first. A player must win 6 games to win a set. In general, to win a match a player must win two out of three sets. A set must be won by a two game margin. In the event of game score of 6-6, a tiebreaker is then played.

# Prologue

"Happy Birthday, Nicole. I can't believe you're already five!" Nicole's dad smiled as he handed her a large beautifully wrapped present.

Nicole quickly tore off the wrapping paper to discover the wooden Chris Everett tennis racquet she had seen in the store.

"Can we *please* go to the park? There's no snow on the ground!" Nicole pleaded with her dad.

"No Honey, it's much too cold outside to play. I promise we'll play as soon as it gets nice outside." her dad replied.

On Saturday, March 17 Nicole woke to a beautiful, sunny day. She felt very lucky. After all, it was St. Patrick's Day. Last evening the weatherman had predicted a sunny day in the mid-60's. Nicole jumped out of bed and ran through the house, finding her Dad reading the newspaper.

"Dad can we *please* go to the park and play tennis? I can't wait to play with my new racquet!" Nicole pleaded with her dad.

"Sure, let's go!"

At the park, Nicole and her dad warmed up slowly, and hit tentatively. After about a half-hour, they got 'in a groove' and started rallying back and forth, just as they regularly had last fall, until it had become too cold to play outdoors.

Her Dad looked across the court and said, "Nicole, today I'm going to teach you a two-handed backhand. This stroke will help you gain confidence in your ability to play the game that I know you already love."

# HAVE FUN

## September 1988

The shrieks and screams could be heard from blocks away, as excited children played kickball in the narrow Milwaukee street. A short distance away a school playground housed two older tennis courts with grass-filled cracks and steel mesh netting. At one end was a discolored, dilapidated backboard to rally against. The courts were vacant and, when used by the local kids, were less for tennis than for tag or wiffleball.

Only miles away, at a posh country club in majestic River Hills, children in designer tennis outfits drilled under the guidance of a tennis pro amid his words of encouragement—"Out in front! Follow through, Cynthia. Another great shot, Jimmy!" Several students occupied each of the eight beautiful courts, just adjacent to the sparkling swimming pool and 18-hole golf course.

Not far from the club, the blare of an announcer echoed from the big-screen TV in the library at the Nelson household. The suburban fieldstone home in nearby Glendale measured over 6,000 square feet, with a beautifully sculpted lawn and a U-shaped driveway allowing easy access to the four-car garage.

The nationally televised match between Andrea Phillips and Beth Jenkins for the fourteen-and-under national junior hard-court tennis championship was taking place in San Diego. Henry Nelson, eagerly into the match, followed every point. Daughter Erin, thirteen, glanced over casually out of a high-back leather chair as she peeked through a teen magazine.

"Erin—did you see that shot? She is an unbelievable player!"

A housekeeper entered with refreshments. The phone rang. Erin answered, spoke briefly, then hung up.

"Mom won't be home until after six," she announced. "Bay Shore is very crowded. Martha should have dinner ready by then."

"Fine," answered Henry.

The commentators continued to praise Andrea's sheer power and the number of aces she had recorded. Henry made notes as he prepared a strategy for his daughter.

"When we're there next year, it will be so much fun," Henry said. A banker in his late thirties, he had been the top player his junior and senior years at nearby Carroll College. Still obsessed with tennis, he played in a local men's league.

Miles away, at the home of Nicole Harris, the match was also viewed on a small, 14-inch black and white television in the living room. Eleven year old Nicole along with her Grandma, affectionately referred to as Mia, intently watched the match. Nicole's brother, eight year old Jon, was off in his own world, playing with his action heroes on the floor. Hopelessly addicted to tennis, clutching her wooden Chris Everett racquet, Nicole ever so often stood up and swung at a make-believe ball.

Nicole's mom Carol poked her head in from the kitchen. "I hope you don't think you can stay up until ten again practicing your volleys in the basement."

"Okay, Mom," obliged Nicole.

The prized wooden racquet was the last present Nicole received from her dad. He had given it to her on her fifth birthday. A year later—now five years ago—he had died in an auto accident. Nicole had enjoyed playing tennis with her father, but after the accident she had given it up until a year ago. It just didn't seem right without him. She remembered how he used to tuck her into bed. He would tell her to dream of a candy tree. The candy tree was a very special and magical tree. Each time you picked a piece of candy off the tree, another magically appeared.

Located in Milwaukee, the Harris home was modest and cozy. The eleven-hundred square foot home had three tiny bedrooms. Beautiful marigolds, the work of Grandma and Carol, stood in the front below the fieldstone facing. Grandma, now age seventy-two with a thick Polish accent, lived with and helped the family. Nicole's mom generally worked the night shift and every other weekend as a neonatal nurse.

As Carol entered the living room, she handed Nicole a list of chores. She discarded her apron, displaying her nursing uniform. Today she was scheduled to work from three until eleven-thirty.

"Already your weekend to work? Has it been two weeks?" Grandma asked.

Carol nodded as she prepared her bag.

"I guess getting through college didn't guarantee you weekends off!"

"It sure didn't. Please heat up the casserole for dinner, ok?"

Carol leaned down, kissed Nicole and Jon, and headed out the door.

The tennis match concluded. "How appropriate that Andrea finished the match with a crushing ace," remarked the announcers. "Her 6-3, 6-3 victory was very impressive. She is only thirteen—in her first year of this age bracket. There's an excellent chance we may see her again next year in the finals!"

The coverage ended with Andrea being handed a huge trophy. Grandma reminisced, recalling how proud the family had been when Nicole had won the County championship last month. Just like Nicole, she had also been the Milwaukee County, twelve and under tennis champion, some sixty years ago. She wished she could have pursued the game a little more, as she really enjoyed it.

Nicole was so much like her grandma, strong and athletic. As a young girl, Mia had also won the Milwaukee County free-throw championship in 1928—making 22 of 25 free throws. Incredibly, Nicole also won this year's free throw county championship just last winter, making the same total—22 of 25.

Nicole had played in a few twelve-and-under tennis tournaments this past summer and had made great progress in a short time. She had found the formal tennis circuit very competitive. Soon she would join a four-week fall league hosted by a City of Milwaukee Parks and Recreation tennis instructor. She would get help, she hoped, in refining her strokes to enable her to play on the challenge ladder with the better players. She was excited.

Sparked by Mr. Harris' lifetime passion, the entire family loved sports. They looked forward to the Summer Olympics and the TV coverage, only three weeks away. This year the games would be held in Seoul, South Korea.

It was an exciting summer. Besides tennis, Nicole played on her church school's softball team and attended a volleyball camp for a week at local Brown Deer High School. The family, including Gram, spent five days at a summer home on Lake Nagawicka, compliments of Dr. Stanwood, a pediatrician who worked with Carol. Nicole frequently baby-sat for his daughter, seven-year-old Jenny, at their Mequon home. Jenny adored Nicole; and the feeling was mutual.

Before long, it was late August; school would begin soon. It was a sacrifice for the Harrises to send their kids to a parochial school, but Carol's overtime helped to make ends meet. In addition to the tuition, there was a requirement for volunteer time. Gram and Carol helped in any way they could. And even though the required uniform was an additional cost, it helped in the long run. Carol was happy that the uniforms evened the playing field, and eliminated the competition regarding everyday dress.

Nicole's seventh grade at St. Elizabeth was an awesome, outstanding class. Although relatively small in size, with only twenty-eight students; most were very athletic and involved in sports, which made a perfect fit for Nicole. With her already strong tennis serve, the carry-over to volleyball was natural. Being taller than most of her classmates, gave Nicole a distinctive advantage and a strong net game. Basketball and softball met with similar success. Nicole, along with her classmates, rotated from one sport to another, their teams always very competitive.

Playing in leagues and tournaments, Nicole developed camaraderie with both teammates and opponents. Nicole enjoyed her teachers and loved the small parochial school atmosphere. As part of each school day, she attended church and loved to light candles for special intentions and blessings. She enjoyed acting in school plays and had an affinity for angels. Her best friend, Cindy Penn, was a fine athlete in her own right. Even though they lived four miles apart, they visited each other at least twice a week during the summer, most often by bike. On warm summer days they peddled over to Algonquin Park and jumped into the pool.

Cindy wasn't into tennis, but she and Nicole were active in dance. Each year Kate's Dance Studio held a recital at local Dominican High. It was *the* event of the year, followed by a special dinner with Cindy's and Nicole's families. Both girls love Italian food, so the unanimous choice was usually *Mama Mia's,* the favorite local Italian restaurant. Certainly Grandma, "Little Mia", couldn't complain about that name!

Once a month, St. Elizabeth sponsored a Friday-night fish fry. This was always a special event; well attended by most of the parish families, and surrounding neighborhood.

The food was scrumptious, drawing large crowds; with the proceeds going to St. Vincent de Paul, an organization that cared for the poor and needy. Grandma would work all day breading fish and Carol would help serve the dinners. Nicole and Jon enjoyed the time with their friends and the excellent food. After dinner, Nicole and her class members helped clean up. Nicole enjoyed lending a hand and could always be counted on to stay until everything was back in its proper place.

But of all her many activities, Nicole most loved tennis. Her hand-eye coordination and height were distinct advantages. At the tender age of five, Nicole's Dad taught her a two-handed backhand. Of all her tennis skills, this seemed to be her strongest. Up to this time, the only way she could play during the school year was to practice strokes in her basement or hit against the wall at the park.

The new fall league lasted four weeks. Nicole loved every minute. Her young instructor, a college student named Pat, enjoyed Nicole's enthusiasm. Since the program was free, Pat spent most of his time trying to undo the baseball-bat-like swings of the participants and promoted knowledge of the rules. He took Nicole aside several times to work on her forehand, emphasizing that she was using too much wrist and reminded her that she needed more follow-through with her forehand strokes.

As the weather grew cold, the serious players moved indoors to hone their skills. Many played in tournaments around the country. This was not possible for Nicole. The cost was too high, out of the question for her family's meager budget. This didn't deter Nicole. She continued to hit against the board at the park until the balls were too cold to bounce back. At this time, she moved her game inside and worked exclusively in her basement. Nicole checked all the available tennis books out from the local library and continued to learn more about the game she loved to play.

In early November, Nicole's class held a mock election for President of the United States. Weeks later, George Bush was elected defeating Michael Dukakis. The same month, the Beach Boys' hot new single, '*Kokomo*' topped the charts. Nicole's Dad had loved the Beach Boys. Nicole continued to be a huge fan and listened to all her dad's old eight-tracks, still in the basement. When Christmas came, Nicole received tennis balls and Mia had made her several tennis outfits for the summer. Carol gave her Anita Baker's latest hit song, *'Giving You The Best That I Got.'*

Over the holidays, the scores of the indoor junior matches and tournaments were listed in the local paper. Nicole followed the scores of players she knew or previously played. She wished she could have participated, but she was thankful for her other activities. Mia told her that her well roundedness would someday be an asset to her.

In April, spring finally arrived and the weather started to improve, with temperatures once again in the high 50's to mid 60's. Yes, spring was definitely in the Midwest air! News broke that Nintendo started selling Gameboy in Japan. Nicole's brother Jon, was very excited, and hoped to get one.

He asked Carol about doing extra chores around the house. In late April, much loved actress Lucille Ball died. She had been one of Mia's favorite TV personalities, lighting up the *I Love Lucy* show. With every watched episode, Mia's hearty laugh had filled the room.

By May, the tulips were in bloom and soon replaced with marigolds in the front of the Harris home. An awesome sight! Nicole was now once again in the habit of going to the park every day to hit against the wooden backboard. Loud "bonks" could be heard as the ball smacked the backboard and made its way back to Nicole for another return.

One day, Nicole met a man hitting balls against the backboard at the park. He looked familiar and then she remembered; she had recently met him and his wife at church. Mr. Novak re-introduced himself and told Nicole that he was a machinist at the packaging plant just up the road. He was in his early thirties, thin, and very athletic. He and Nicole quickly bonded. Impressed with her drive and hard work ethic, he volunteered to hit with her on a regular basis. Mr. Novak's strokes weren't perfect, but he hustled and hit the ball extremely hard. Nicole in turn, offered him advice about his form, and she realized that she enjoyed sharing tips she had learned from the books she read over the winter. She found when placed in a coaching position, it made her more cognizant and careful to provide accurate information and quickly learned that her own game improved as a result.

Nicole and Mr. Novak continued to hit twice a week,

both benefitted from the practice. He provided Nicole with greater strength, quickness, and reaction time than players her age. Nicole continued to offer suggestions to him, improving his form and approach to the game. Due to her practice with Mr. Novak and from all the books that she had eagerly read, Nicole started to develop a solid understanding of tennis.

"Where did you get that backhand? It's unbelievable!" Mr. Novak asked one day.

"I owe my backhand to a great teacher, who continues to watch over me like a guardian angel!" Nicole replied with a smile.

# ASSUME A READY POSITION

The school year was coming to a close and mid-May brought Nicole her first tennis tournament of the season. She was so excited to compete and happy that the tournament didn't interfere with her softball schedule. Since Carol had to work the first two days, Mia agreed to drive and provide moral support. Mr. Novak wished Nicole luck, told her to have fun and encouraged her to do her best.

On Friday evening, Mia and Nicole drove out to Hartland for the Lake Country Open, which was held in a beautiful indoor facility. Since this tournament coincided with a national tournament in Kalamazoo, Michigan, the draw was limited. Many of the better players were away, out of state, and only two of the top players from last year, Terry Williams and Colleen Henderson, attended. Terry was seeded number one and Colleen number two. Nicole wore one of the outfits that she had received for Christmas from Mia. She was eager to play.

Nicole's first match started out slowly and she quickly realized that her match play was rusty. Her opponent, Delafield's Pam Lewis, had great strokes, but Nicole hustled for every point. As the match went on, Nicole noticed that Pam's backhand was considerably weaker. Nicole recalled reading in one of the many tennis books, to attack the weaknesses of the opponent. Using this information, Nicole consciously started to aim her shots to Pam's backhand whenever possible. The strategy proved successful and the match turned around quickly. Nicole won 6-4, 6-1.

On Saturday at 10:00 a.m. Nicole was scheduled to meet the number-two seed. While not yet state-ranked, Colleen was one of the best thirteen-year-olds in the Hartland area with a hard first serve and great form. On Saturday, Mia once again drove Nicole to Hartland. Jon came along to cheer on Nicole. Nicole felt confident, even though she knew she was up against a strong opponent. The evening before, Mia and Nicole had stayed to watch the end of Colleen's match. Nicole felt she was up to the challenge, having played a solid opening-round match and started to feel more comfortable on the indoor courts.

As Nicole and Colleen made their way out onto the court, Nicole walked past Gram.

"Court Four, Mia!" she smiled, and displayed the tennis balls that showed Penn 4.

Mia knew that Nicole's favorite number was four, the same as her Dad's. Mia smiled back. "An omen?" she replied.

The match was closer than most people anticipated. Thanks to her practice with Mr. Novak, Nicole was able to return most of the serves by blocking the ball. She hustled and ran down every ball. Nicole won the first set, 6-4. With Colleen serving at 4-5, ad-out in the second set, Colleen hit her first serve into the net. Nicole prepared for the second. It came, a spin  serve that pulled Nicole off the court, as Colleen charged the net. Nicole took a chance and hit the ball cross-court and short. Colleen lunged, catching the ball on the short bounce just off the ground. The ball sailed off her racquet and into the top of net. Nicole won, and was now in the semi-finals.

The girls met at the net and shook hands. As they stepped to the tournament desk, Colleen started to cry. Nicole told Colleen she felt lucky to beat her.

"You're a great player, the best I've ever played!"

Colleen told Nicole that she thought that she would easily make it to the finals, since four of the top five from the state were absent.

With two hours until the next match, Jon, Nicole, and Mia settled on a couch in the corner and ate the sandwiches and fruit Mia had prepared for the trip. The number-one seed, Terry Williams, was on the other side of the draw. If Nicole won her next match, she would face Terry in the final.

At 2:00 sharp, the desk called Nicole's name, along with Julie Adams, her opponent. Even though she wasn't sent to Court Four, she was handed Penn 4's. After the girls finished their ten-minute warm-up, they spun a racquet to determine who would serve. Julie won.

Like Nicole, Julie was relatively new to tennis tournament play. Both girls displayed great hustle, but a trained tennis eye could see that both players' strokes needed work. Nonetheless, it was an exciting match. The momentum shifted almost every game. It went to a third set, as Julie won the first, 6-4, and Nicole the second, 7-5. Nicole broke Julie's serve twice, to take a 5-3 lead. The last game reached deuce three times before Nicole hit a cross-court winner followed by a topspin lob to seal the victory.

Nicole was elated as she made her way to the desk. It

was only her first tournament of the year, and she felt blessed to be in the finals. Nicole had never come close to reaching the finals of a big tournament before. Yes, she won the Milwaukee County Twelve's last year, but all the players had been novices without any real tennis experience. This final would be a true test, as she would face last year's number-seven player in the state. Terry Williams had been on the circuit for more than four years. She took tennis seriously and had private lessons twice a week. She and Erin Nelson had gone to the Western Sectionals last year as first-year 14's. She was expected to be in the top three this year.

The finals were scheduled for Sunday, Carol's day off. Consequently, the entire family planned to attend. They arrived in Hartland a half hour early. Carol was excited to see Nicole play for the first time this year. As the director announced their names, Terry and Nicole stepped up to the desk. Terry and Nicole introduced themselves to each other. Nicole noticed that Terry was covered with sweat. She told Nicole that she had been warming up for an hour with her pro.

After the girls took the court and engaged in a ten-minute warm-up, the match began. The first two games were played evenly. Then Terry took control, and with her powerful ground strokes, broke Nicole down. Gradually Terry worked her way to the net in order to angle volleys for points. Terry then hit several winners off Nicole's second serve. Nicole fought back with all she had, but Terry's strokes and control gave her a distinct advantage. The match ended 6-2, 6-3.

Nicole was very dejected. As they approached the desk, Nicole was greeted by her family, and Terry by her tennis pro. Terry was awarded the first-place trophy, Nicole the second-place.

On the way home, the Harrises consoled Nicole and reminded her that she had met a very solid, tough opponent. Everyone told Nicole that she played very well and were all proud of her efforts and the result. After all, finishing second, in such a high level tournament was a great accomplishment. While Carol had never played tennis, Mia had, and she could see what the difference was—it had nothing to do with effort.

"If you break it down, some girls have years more experience than their opponents, even though they are the same age," Mia remarked analytically. "As a result, they have better perfected strokes, which results in more confidence. This in itself, can be very intimidating to tennis newcomers. Nicole, we're proud of you. You played well. The difference is practice. You'll catch up, if you continue to work hard and believe in yourself."

Mia's encouragement was just what Nicole needed to hear to overcome her sadness from her defeat. Nicole took the pep talk to heart and felt a renewed sense of resolve and determination. The somber mood shifted and soon everyone felt like celebrating. The family stopped at Kopps in Brookfield for giant hamburgers and ice-cream cones for desert.

On Tuesday, Nicole met Mr. Novak at the scheduled

time. He was excited to hear about the tournament results from Nicole's perspective.

"Just think, you could be a ranked player by the end of the summer if we keep hitting. And I can enter my first men's tournament!"

"That would be a great goal for both of us," replied Nicole.

The following day, Nicole's softball team won the league. She was the pitcher in a fast-pitch league. She thought that pitching would help her gain arm strength for the tennis circuit. Being so stroke-conscious in tennis, Nicole became so in her other sports as well. Her excellent technique made her a great hitter in baseball. Everyone complimented Nicole on her smooth swing. From early on, her Dad had worked with her and taught her how to hit a baseball—elbow up and swing level. Nicole thought it funny that she had one of the best swings in softball but had never received such a compliment about her tennis, especially about her forehand. Tennis players with great strokes always seemed to rank high or very high. She wondered how she could improve her strokes quickly. The state-closed junior qualifying tournament was scheduled for late June, only six weeks away. From this tournament she could become a ranked player and possibly even qualify for the sectional, in Michigan. For it to become a reality, she knew she needed to re-dedicate herself and improve dramatically.

Nicole's family was in agreement. Nicole could play the five necessary tournaments to become a ranked player, but no more. Everyone realized that it would be time-consuming, and require travel and money; but it was what Nicole truly wanted. In addition to the state-closed, Nicole needed to play three additional tournaments. After reviewing the tournament schedule, she decided to play the three before the state-closed, to have maximum experience by that time. Her family agreed that the plan made sense, since the Closed Tournament was arguably the most important. The top players in the state-closed qualified for the Western Sectional Tournament in East Lansing, Michigan. From there, players could advance to the national junior hard-court championships in San Diego—the tournament Nicole had so eagerly watched Andrea Phillips win on television last summer.

At the end of May, Nicole entered her next tournament. This one was held in Kohler, Wisconsin, about 65 miles north of the Harris home. This popular event featured seventeen players in the girls' fourteens. Nicole's mom had the weekend off, so the whole family attended. Play was scheduled to start on Saturday morning. For those who advanced, two matches were scheduled to be played each day.

An hour before Nicole's 10:00 match, the Harrises arrived at the club, a gorgeous facility offering eight indoor and sixteen outdoor tennis courts. When they checked in at the desk, Nicole was surprised to hear the director, Ed Simmons comment, "So you're Nicole Harris. I heard about your fine showing in Hartland."

"Thank you. It was a lot of fun."

"Well, we're glad to have you here."

The Harris' made their way over to the draw, displayed on an easel. Four players were seeded. Number 1 was Erin Nelson from Glendale; number 2, Sara Cummings; number 3, Lindsey Smith; and number 4, Dawn Anderson. Nicole's first match paired her against Angie Martin from nearby Sheboygan. All the matches were scheduled to be played on the indoor courts.

At 10:00 sharp, Angie and Nicole took the court and warmed up. The match began. The first two games were close, knotting the girls at 1-1. From there, Nicole started to play with more confidence, and seemed to elevate her game, which served to put additional pressure on Angie. Extremely consistent from the baseline, Nicole appeared to win every rally. The match ended quickly, with Nicole decisively overcoming Angie, 6-2, 6-1.

As she made her way to the desk, Nicole walked past Erin Nelson, the top player in the state. Nicole had seen her play last year. "Hi," each said, as they crossed paths. Nice match," said Erin, and "Thanks," Nicole replied. At the tournament desk, the director informed Nicole, her next match was scheduled for 2:00. Since Sara Cummings, the number-two seed, had already won, Nicole was told she would meet Sara in the next round. Sara was a great player. Last year, she finished seventh in the fourteen and under division. The girls ahead of her had moved up to the sixteen and under division this year, except for Erin Nelson, the number-one seed in the Kohler tournament, and Terry Williams.

The Harris family left to get some lunch. With two hours until the next match, they took a leisurely drive. They enjoyed the ride, taking in the picturesque hillside and farms which added to the scenic beauty of the area, on this sunny day. At Culvers, a local custard diner, they enjoyed a lunch of burgers and the custard of the day, mint chocolate chip cones. They discussed the tournament, and Nicole's next match. Everyone knew Nicole was paired against a great player. Carol told Nicole, "Have fun out there! Playing a good player can bring out your best. Make the most of it!" It went unsaid, that a loss this afternoon meant a long trip home, with no need to return tomorrow. Until the semi-finals, this tournament was single elimination.

They checked in at the desk with plenty of time to spare. Sara and her parents were already there. The girls received their balls and walked together to the court. In the warm-up, they lost track of time. They were both hitting the ball well, with few errors. After fifteen minutes, the tournament director told them to start their match. Nicole spun her racquet and won the right to serve.

The match was not disappointing. Both girls continued the high level of play that had started in the warm-up. Both appeared determined to keep the ball in play, to not miss a shot. With the score tied 4-4, Nicole played confidently and continued to hustle, as always. Sara, whose strokes were near picture perfect, became visibly frustrated when Nicole continued to return every ball sent her way. Sara started talking to herself, and banged her racquet after missed shots.

Soon Sara's errors started to pile up, and Nicole seemed to have an answer for each shot at the right time. She won the first set by a 7-5 margin.

Sara came back aggressively. She would not give in without a battle. With Nicole up 6-5 in the second set and the score at 30-30, Sara served her second serve and Nicole took a chance. She cut at the ball and dropped her return just over the net. Sara sprinted toward the ball, but had no chance. She yelled and slapped her side in frustration.

It was now match point. Sara's first serve struck the bottom of the net. She sighed deeply, and spun her second serve. The ball hit the net and bounced off the court—double fault.

Nicole ran to the net extending her hand to Sara. But Sara, fuming, refused to acknowledge Nicole. Instead, she walked quickly to the bench by her bag, sat down and folded her arms. Nicole retrieved her water jug and walked over to Sara. "Nice match, Sara," she said, and headed to the tournament desk.

Nicole made it to the semis, giving the Harris family a great reason to return on Sunday. Nicole also felt better because the twenty-five-dollar tournament fee was now for four matches—the most she could get, definitely their money's worth. As Nicole reported the match score to the tournament desk, Sara's mother approached Carol.

"What kind of racquet does your daughter use?" she asked harshly.

Carol smiled. "A Chris Everett," she relied. "It was only

$19.99. I can even tell you where we got it."

"That's ridiculous. Get with the *times.*"

And the woman stormed off.

On the way home, Carol shared her experience but didn't understand what happened. Nicole explained that almost all the players were using graphite racquets with a much larger head or "sweet spot" than the wooden one she was using. In fact, most usually had several on hand in their bags.

Mia laughed. "And you thought you were going to help the lady save some money!"

Nicole just beat her first ranked opponent. She felt like she belonged. As the Harrises made their way toward the car, Mr. Nelson, Erin's father, walked up to Nicole.

"Nicole you played great, you're really coming along. Who do you take lessons with?" he asked.

"Mr. Novak."

"Who? I've … never heard of him."

# PLAY THE BALL,
# NOT THE OPPONENT

To make it to Kohler a half-hour before the 10:00 match, the Harrises had to get up early. They ate a quick breakfast, attended St. Elizabeth's 7:30 Mass, and ducked out a bit early.

Another beautiful day unfolded. This was an open tournament, which meant girls from anywhere, even outside the state, could participate. After beating the number-two seed, Nicole's next opponent was Angie Martin from Chicago. She was a second-year 14's player ranked both in Illinois and in the section. Last year, she finished behind Erin and Terry in the Midwest section and therefore was seeded behind them in this tournament.

The previous match finished early, and Angie and Nicole took the indoor court to warm up. Spectators could view from one end right above the court. A crowd gathered. Nicole spotted Mr. Nelson and Erin. Erin was slated for the other semi-final which had not yet started play.

Nicole won the racquet flip, and suddenly felt 'butterflies' in her stomach. She was unaccustomed to playing before such a large audience. She hesitated, said a short prayer, and asked for strength to maintain her concentration.

Angie yelled over , "Are you okay?"

"Just fine," replied Nicole as she lined up to serve. The first serve missed wide right. Since she didn't have a true spin serve, her second serve was much like the first, but she took a little off to insure its accuracy. Immediately, Angie took advantage of this lesser offering and hit the ball hard, but just outside the court.

Nicole sighed with relief, and lined up for the second point. She had to get her first serve in or prepare for an onslaught. Her next serve hit the inside line of the service box. Angie lunged. The tip of her racquet hit the ball squarely into the net. Nicole was up 30-0 and had yet to hit a groundstroke.

"Let's go, Angie!" called her parents.

Nicole served. The ball came off her racquet with power and hit deep on the inside of the box. Angie couldn't even get to the ball—an ace, the first of Nicole's career. As she readied herself with the score 40-0, Nicole noticed Angie retreating on the court. Nicole then hit a second serve to the middle of the box. She thought that keeping Angie off balance might make up for her less-powerful second serve. Angie rushed up; returned the ball. Now, for the first time in the match, the two were rallying. The ball went back and forth nearly twenty times before Nicole's baseline shot hit the top of the net and dropped abruptly over onto Angie's side for the point, and first game.

"That's the worst game I've ever played," said Angie, as the two changed sides.

"I got pretty lucky," said Nicole.

The match grew very competitive. The lead did not change by more than one game the first set. Both girls were hitting terrifically. Points were difficult to come by. Nicole was playing the best she ever had. Her ability to block Angie's serve really kept her in the match. Ahead, 6-5, and the score 30-40, Nicole prepared to receive serve. Angie smacked a serve right at Nicole's feet. With no time to react, Nicole stuck out her racquet to block the ball. The ball arched high and over the net at about the middle of the court. Knowing she had hit a great serve, Angie rushed the net, but then took pause. The return was longer than she had anticipated. She reached up for an overhead, her only possibility now. She touched the ball lightly, sending it looping short just over the net. Nicole ran up, let the weak return hit the court and bounce and as the ball moved back up into an advantageous position, hit a winner to the corner.

Nicole won the first set, 7-5. Angie stood dejected as Nicole began to serve. As Nicole readied herself, Angie moved off the court, as if to say she was not ready. Mysteriously, she did this several times during the second set. Each time Nicole waited patiently for her to get set and continued. Nicole was not angry or distracted by this tactic and maintained her poise the entire match. Conversely, it seemed that Angie grew more upset every time the delay tactic didn't seem to phase Nicole. Playing her very best, Nicole won the second set by a decisive 6-3 margin.

An elated Nicole returned to the desk and greeted her waiting family. Mr. Nelson and Erin were also at the desk as she reported her score, and congratulated Nicole. After checking the draw, Nicole noted that Erin had easily won her match, 6-1, 6-1. The final was scheduled for 2:00 and both players were requested to return no later than 1:45. Mom, Gram, and Jon all hugged Nicole, and told her she played a great match.

Gram complimented Nicole stating, "I'm so proud that

you didn't let Angie's stall tactics affect your game! That kind of composure is what makes a great player greater!"

The Harrises again chose to eat at Culver's restaurant, the local favorite. Gram said that it was her treat, since her number-one granddaughter had played so well. Carol wondered why Mr. Nelson had watched most of Nicole's match instead of watching his own daughter Erin's.

"Maybe he was doing a little scouting for the final!" Mia commented.

Everyone enjoyed lunch and the caramel pecan custard cones for dessert. Nicole returned to the club rested and well fed.

Both girls took the court at precisely 1:45. Nicole understood that she now faced the hands-down top girl in the state, if not in the section. Erin had been third in the state last year. The two girls above her moved to the 16's division. In the sectionals, Erin had finished fourteenth, good enough to get her into the national hard-court tournament. However, after returning home from Michigan last summer, she had fallen ill and had to forfeit her spot. The family had been upset. The national tournament in San Diego had been their collective dream.

Erin was far friendlier than many of the other fine players Nicole had faced.

"I was sorry to hear that you were sick last year and couldn't play in the nationals," Nicole sympathetically told Erin.

"Yeah," Erin replied. "That was a bummer; a really

crummy way to end the year!"

The two warmed up for the designated ten minutes, and then spun for the serve. By now a fairly large crowd had convened, peering down onto the court. The match for the championship was soon underway.

Erin and Nicole were both hitting well. Erin had fine control of her shots and the ability to answer any threat with the proper response. Up to this point, many of Nicole's opponents would hit the ball hard and hope it would go in. Erin's game was a major upgrade from such a "spray and pray" approach. Erin quickly took control of the match, opening up a 5-1 lead. Nicole continued to work hard, but Erin's experience proved too much. On several of Nicole's shots, Erin would call "Great shot!" or Nice hit, Nicole!" This was unique. Most opponents had never shown such sportsmanship. After an hour and twenty minutes, Erin won, 6-2, 6-2. Nicole just finished playing the top girl in the state, perhaps the section. Nicole knew that she played her best, without intimidation. Erin confirmed to Nicole that it was possible to be a great player and display good sportsmanship. Most importantly, Nicole felt she had made a friend. She respected Erin Nelson very much.

After the match, Erin hugged Nicole and praised her effort. As they neared the desk, both girls were smiling. After receiving their trophies, the two met with their families, to kisses and hugs.

"I really had a lot of fun, even though I lost," said Nicole.

"That's the spirit, Nicole!" said Mia.

Erin approached. "Nicole, my doubles partner didn't show up. I was wondering—would you be able to play with me? There won't be any extra cost."

Nicole looked to her mother. "Can I Mom, please?" she said.

"Sure thing. It sounds like fun."

Since there were only four teams and Erin and Nicole were top-seeded, to win the doubles tournament would only require two matches; one right after the other. Nicole had only played doubles once before. It was a welcome change. There wasn't nearly as much individual pressure and she had a teammate to confide in.

The matches were truly enjoyable. With Erin's generous coaching, Nicole quickly came to understand her role and court tactics. The girls devised hand signals to display behind their backs to communicate their strategy. They were a delight to watch. On many of their points, they high-fived each other or touched racquets as a sign of unity and celebration. They laughed at their mistakes and complimented their opponents. What a difference from singles play, where each player was on her own and the pressure all hers.

The girls both played well. After winning both matches by scores of 6-1, 6-3 and 6-4, 6-2, Nicole and Erin received the first-place trophies. Before leaving, the two exchanged phone numbers and discovered that they actually lived only a few miles apart. Erin told Nicole that her family had their own court. As the Harrises headed back to Milwaukee, everyone agreed that it had been a wonderful, magical day. Not only had Nicole played extremely well, but she had made a new friend.

# BI-SECT THE ANGLE
# OF THE BALL

Nicole's softball team continued to play well, and went on to win the championship. Nicole, Cindy, and two other teammates were named to the all-star team. It was almost a week before Nicole was able to hit again with Mr. Novak. He was elated to hear about the Kohler tournament and Nicole's softball. His tennis game, too, was improving. He said that he was considering entering a tournament soon. Nicole had only two more tournaments to go before the all-important state closed. Her next would be in Janesville, Wisconsin.

Two days before the tournament, Erin invited Nicole to her house to play tennis and swim. They played tennis for about an hour. Erin's dad came out to observe and offered some pointers. The Nelson backyard was beautiful, with an abundance of trees and flowers lining the court. A trampoline provided a new adventure for Nicole. The girls had a great time in the pool and then leisurely tanned on rafts, the color and shape of a tennis ball.

"The rafts were my Dad's idea," Erin said.

They were made a bit small. That was his only double fault," she chuckled with her pun.

After the swim, Martha served lunch on the patio. With his wife out shopping, Mr. Nelson joined them. Nicole told Erin that she had entered the Janesville tournament.

"Are you going to play in Janesville, Erin?" Nicole asked her friend.

"No, I won't be going to Janesville on Saturday. I'm playing in a tournament in Naperville, Illinois, and will be gone all weekend." Erin replied.

After lunch, the girls hung around in Erin's room. Erin's room was quite large with a queen-size bed and a lot of tennis memorabilia. In one corner stood a chair shaped like a tennis racquet. A matching ottoman appeared like a tennis ball. A poster of Jennifer Capriati hung on the wall, beside a list of goals for the upcoming season. Circled and written in a special pink color was the national tournament.

Erin reached up and pulled a book off her bookshelf. She handed Nicole a book, published by the Wisconsin Tennis Association.

"Nicole have you ever seen this before?" Erin asked.

Nicole shook her head.

"People refer to this as the tennis bible!" Erin laughed as she explained. "It's a yearly almanac that ranks people from Wisconsin for the state, sectional, and national levels for all divisions, both girls and boys. Based on yearly results against other players, each player is positioned accordingly."

As Nicole studied the book, she noted that Erin was ranked number three in the state girls 14's; and ranked 14th in the western section. Erin's picture was in the book. Nicole never realized how structured junior tennis was, and was only beginning to understand the ranking system. Erin wasn't bragging. She was trying to help Nicole learn the system. After about an hour Carol arrived to pick up Nicole. Pulling away from the large home, Carol confessed to Nicole that she felt a little uncomfortable pulling up to the Nelson's home in a tiny Corolla.

"But I like our car. It's us," replied Nicole with a smile.

On Saturday morning, Nicole, Mia and Jon headed for Janesville, a small town about 30 miles south of Madison for the "Barrel of Fun" Tournament. The trip took about an hour and a half. Carol was disappointed that she had to work; she really enjoyed watching Nicole play tennis. As soon as they arrived, they checked in. Nicole was given a tournament T-shirt, customary at many of the smaller, local tournaments. Oftentimes, the players would change into the clean T-shirt for subsequent matches. They quickly went over to peruse the posted draw to see who was playing in the tournament.

Nicole was surprised to see that for the first time ever, she was seeded—number two. The number-one seed, Heidi Miller from Janesville, had been the state's tenth-ranked player last year. There were fourteen players in the tournament. Since Heidi and Nicole were seeded, both had a 'bye' for the first round. At 12:00, Nicole was scheduled to play her opening match against Debra Welling from Madison. Debra had already won her 8:00 match over Tammy Davis, 6-4, 6-4. The tournament was held outside, and Nicole was assigned to Court Four. As Nicole made her way she said to Mia, "Court Four." Gram once again nodded and smiled.

After the finals of the Kohler tournament just one week earlier, the match seemed low-key. Nonetheless, Nicole knew she had to play tough. No one would just lie down and play dead just because she was seeded. Besides, how had Erin played Nicole? She had displayed good sportsmanship and led by example. Nicole felt Erin was a great role model and decided to copy her good example. After all, Nicole felt very privileged to be seeded and wanted to play her best to demonstrate to the tournament directors that they were justified in her seeding.

Nicole started quickly, on top of her game, moving to a 5-1 lead. While Debra lacked Nicole's consistency, she was a hustler. She stormed back to tie the score 5-5, after Nicole hit several shots wide from the baseline and hit two double faults. Nicole knew she was the stronger player, but found herself being outplayed. How quickly things can change in a week! She knew she needed to concentrate; and the time was now.

Nicole quickly put together a string—twelve straight points—ending with an ace on the final point. Only after she won the first set 7-5 and was up 1-0 in the second set did Debra finally break her game streak. Nicole once again came back, and even reached the net three times with successful volleys. She won the match 7-5, 6-2

Now in the semifinals, Nicole could rest until tomorrow. While many of the families chose to stay overnight in Janesville, the Harrises' limited budget prompted them to drive the hour and a half home. They took their time and enjoyed the picturesque beauty of the Wisconsin farmlands. With Nicole slated to play Sunday at 10:00, the family chose to attend Saturday night Mass. This would give them more time in the morning. At church, Nicole and Jon saw some of their school friends and stopped to talk with them.

Nicole's classmate Luann mentioned she had seen Nicole's name in the paper about the Kohler tournament.

A shocked Nicole responded, "Really?" and Jon added, "My big sister was a seed this weekend in Janesville."

Nicole quickly jumped in. "There aren't many ranked players there, so I kind of lucked out."

At home, the Harrises had a picnic supper of Jello, potato salad, pickles, and hamburgers made on their Weber grill. This was a feast the family always enjoyed. Carol was scheduled to work the night shift, but had slept peacefully all day. She was the designated griller, a task her husband had always enjoyed. After dinner, Carol kissed the kids goodnight, offered Nicole encouragement and 'good luck' for tomorrow's matches. She would not be home by the time they left.

At 8:00 Mia, Jon, and Nicole left for Janesville. It was another beautiful, summer day. The morning sun felt wonderful as they drove back to Janesville.

Nicole checked in and learned she would play Julie Knox from Ripon, Wisconsin. The girls took the court precisely at 10:00. Nicole was really psyched. She desperately wanted to finally win a state sanctioned girls 14's tournament. It would be so great to surprise Mom with the news! She knew it was Mom's hard work and struggle that made this possible. Yesterday, Nicole over-heard some of the older players talking about earning full tennis scholarships to college and having the ability to travel. She decided then and there to work harder and to set even higher goals.

The match was very competitive. From the baseline Julie was like a backboard. While her ability to return almost every ball was her greatest strength, her problem areas were her serve and lack of an accomplished net game. Nicole ended up losing the first set 6-4.

Nicole found herself looking for answers and needed them in a hurry. She decided on a strategy to mix the game up a bit, in order to force Julie to hit a wider variety of shots. Nicole charged the net to force Julie to make quicker, well-placed returns. Nicole also hit several under-spin shots which drew Julie to the net and forced her to put up lazy shots. This allowed Nicole to lob or pass her successfully. The strategy worked perfectly, and Nicole turned the match around. She won the second set 6-2, and the third 6-3.

This was Nicole's second three-set match of the year and with this victory, she was now in the finals, which were set for 2:00. Mia, Jon, and Nicole went into town for hotdogs. With the other semi-final just starting its second set, they had plenty of time. Top seed Heidi Miller had won the first set 6-3. Jumbo dogs were a family favorite. Jon loved to put absolutely everything on them including cheese and sauerkraut. The condiments were a family joke as Jon's hot dog was always twice the size of anyone else's.

"Jon—are you sure there's a hot dog in there?" Mia asked.

Nicole changed for the second match. The fresh clothes felt good. She also changed her headband, quite damp from her sweat, and when she took her headband off she noticed a distinct ring on her forehead from the sun. Mia said it looked as if she still had her headband on. Grandma suggested that she also wear a visor, since the sun can be very damaging to your skin.

Leisurely they finished lunch and took their time returning. They stopped at the draw to see how the Miller match had gone. There was surprising news. Heidi had suffered a turned ankle and had been unable to continue the second set, awarding her opponent the victory. Consequently, Nicole was scheduled to meet Beth Colby from Waukesha, instead of Heidi, in the finals.

Nicole spotted Heidi under a tree, her foot wrapped with ice and her family around her. Nicole walked over, bent down, and told her how sorry she was.

"Thanks Nicole," replied Heidi. "Just make sure you play your best and get the victory."

"Thanks Heidi, I'll do my best," answered Nicole.

In theory, Nicole had been handed a great gift since she would not have to play a seed in the final. On the one hand, she hoped for the win; but on the other hand, the victory would be less meaningful in terms of rankings. She understood this, but her real dilemma was that she wanted to feel that she truly earned a first place trophy, by beating a seeded opponent. When she told Mia how she felt, Mia said, "Nicole, isn't this the same situation Erin faced when she played you in the Kohler tournament? She thought she would have to face a seed, but ended up playing you?"

"Wow, Gram, you're right," said Nicole. "I didn't even

think of that."

Nicole felt better. Besides, she promised Heidi she would play her best!

Nicole approached the desk and introduced herself to Beth. The two girls took the court a little after 2:00. The afternoon grew hotter—into the 90's. Nicole soon felt sweaty even in her fresh outfit.

Gram and Jon found a shady spot to watch, and after a ten-minute warm-up, the match began. Nicole was determined to get a solid start, and did just that. The first seven points were hers before she hit a forehand wide to the right. In less than a half-hour she had a commanding 5-1 lead. She rose to the occasion and hit with real authority, painting the lines. She couldn't believe her accuracy and lack of errors, and played with newfound confidence. Even though her opponent wasn't the seed she had hoped to beat, she was still formidable, consistently keeping the ball deep and never quit. Nicole played consistently. Now in the second set, she worked to get to the net, a part of her game that needed development. This was an opportune time to work on her net game. Although she won fewer points, she gained added confidence and a greater understanding of when and how to approach the net.

The match ended; Nicole was victorious with scores of 6-1 and 6-3. The match was over in a short one hour and fifteen minutes. She met Beth at the net. Beth told Nicole that she deserved the victory.

"You're a great player, Nicole." Beth generously

shared.

"I was very lucky I hit the ball so well today," Nicole replied. Then added, "You really do a great job keeping the ball deep."

Nicole received her trophy; her first tournament victory on the junior circuit. It was a very special day and a tournament that Nicole would never forget. Mia and Jon hugged Nicole.

"We're very proud of you, little one!" Mia said. "It was all your hard work that earned this trophy."

The ride home was very pleasant. Nicole couldn't wait to see Mom. As they pulled the car into the driveway, Carol came running out to out to greet them.

"Well—how did you do? What happened? Tell me quickly, I can't stand the suspense any longer!"

Nicole opened the car door and handed the trophy to her mom, and pointed to the "first place!"

"Wow!" Carol yelled.

"Mom, thanks for giving me the opportunity to play in these tournaments. I really appreciate it."

Carol gave her a big hug. With that, they walked into the house to a wonderfully prepared shrimp salad and hot French bread.

On Monday, Nicole played with her best friend in the neighborhood, Carrie Grover. Since none of the local kids played junior tennis or understood its complexities, Nicole didn't even mention a word about her exciting weekend. The girls biked to Plaid Pantry for some candy, then rode back to Carrie's house and ate on the back porch. Carrie and her mother were going shopping at noon, so Nicole went home. Besides, Mia wanted Nicole home for lunch, because afterwards she needed to do her chores on Mom's list.

On Tuesday, Nicole met Mr. Novak at the regular time. He was so surprised, but pleased to hear about Nicole's victory.

"Thank you, Mr. Novak, if it wasn't for you, I wouldn't be doing this well," Nicole gratefully told him.

They played until it got too dark to see the ball. He walked Nicole the four blocks to her home and finally had the opportunity to formally meet the Harris family.

"I've heard so much about you. Thank you for practicing with Nicole. We all appreciate your help," Carol said.

"I'm the one who should be thanking you. Nicole is such a breath of fresh air. She has been the one giving me lessons, if you can believe that!"

They sat and talked for a short while longer and ended the night enjoying some cherry pie that Mia had freshly baked that afternoon.

Wednesday night was the all-star softball game. Nicole put on her St. Elizabeth uniform, grabbed her glove, and headed out. She had to be at the field forty-five minutes early for batting practice. At the designated time, she met her 'new team', the all-stars from her entire league. Nicole was so glad that her dear friend Cindy was on her team. Nicole started at first base, Cindy at second. After two innings, Nicole replaced the starting pitcher, Natasha and pitched the next two innings.

Mia, Carol, and Jon attended. The game was exciting. With Nicole's team up to bat last in the bottom of the seventh-inning, the game was tied 8-8 with two outs and Cindy on second base. Nicole came up to bat. The first pitch was high. The next was right down the middle. Nicole swung and fouled off the ball high and to the first base side, landing very near her family, who jumped out of the way to avoid being beaned.

"Sorry, guys!" she yelled, to bring a general burst of laughter.

Nicole re-gripped the bat, raised her elbow, and readied herself. The pitch came, right in the strike  zone, and Nicole swung. The ball rocketed solidly off the bat into right center field. Sure that the ball had made its way past the infield, Cindy sprinted off. Her third-base coach, Mr. Krupo, signaled her to make the turn and head for home. The ball was cleanly fielded, with a solid relay to the shortstop. Her throw to the plate was accurate. Her teammates all yelled for Cindy to slide. It would be very close. Cindy hit the ground, slid in a huge cloud of dust, just as the ball arrived. The umpire viewed the play for a second, then yelled— "Safe!"

Nicole's team erupted. They had won.

Afterwards, both teams lined up and congratulated each other.   Cindy's dad insisted on taking the Harrises to Kopps, the local custard stand for an ice cream celebration.  As they put their order in, Cindy looked like a walking ad for a detergent commercial. The girls didn't care. They won; and wore their dirty uniforms as a badge of honor. They knew it was all for the cause.

The following weekend there was no tournament. Nicole spent the weekend hitting with Mr. Novak, against the back board at the park, and working on her second serve. She was having a difficult time perfecting her second serve, a serve calling for more spin. She wondered how so many of the other players picked up and mastered this technique.

Nicole's summer calendar was certainly filled. From one sport or event to the next, Nicole was constantly busy. Next weekend would already be Nicole's last tournament before the all-important Wisconsin State Closed. Her annual dance recital was scheduled for the end of June. Baseball was over for the year, but volleyball camp was planned for the end of June. Finally, the Harris family annual vacation week on Lake Nagawicka, thanks to Dr. Stanwood, was set for the end of August.

On Friday night, Carrie spent the night with Nicole. The girls enjoyed planning 'sleep-overs' together; and this one was no exception. The girls rented two movies. Jon liked spending time with the girls, especially when they had movies. The girls never minded. They just made more popcorn. They loved to play music and dance to popular songs. "Love Shack" by the B-52's, "Pump Up The Jam" by Technotronic Feat Felly, and "Bust A Move" by Young MC were hits with the girls. As for Nicole, her personal favorite was "The Wind Beneath Your Wings" by Bett Midler. The song seemed to touch her, deeply. She had used her baby-sitting money to buy the song to play over and over.

# UTILIZE PROPER FOOTWORK

The week flew by. The weekend arrived and Nicole felt ready for the Waukesha Open, the last tournament before the biggest tournament of the season, the Wisconsin Closed. Carol was happy that the tournament was scheduled on her weekend off. She drove the family the short twenty-mile distance to the Waukesha Open. Nicole's first match was slated to start at 11:00. Last week, Erin told Nicole that she decided on the last minute to play in the tournament.

Minutes after arriving, Nicole learned she was scheduled to play Lucy Evans from Tucson, Arizona. Nicole was seeded, but fourth. Erin was seeded number one, and Terry Williams, number two. Number three, Susan Minifie, had been ranked last year and had won an indoor tournament in the spring, beating Sara Cummings. With only twelve girls in the tournament, all the seeds drew byes for the first round, which started last night. Nicole spotted Erin, and they agreed to warm-up together.

Erin asked Nicole, "Do you know about the Gunthermans?" Nicole shook her head, and Erin explained, "They come from Madison for many of the tournaments and have two girls, Ann in the 14's and Jenny in the 16's. They always bring their huge motor home. It's sitting right there."

Nicole looked over. A huge Winnebago stood parked.

"Whenever people come to the tournament they always say, Oh, the Gunthermans are here!"

Nicole laughed. "I think I saw that big vehicle in Kohler,"

she said.

Erin grinned. "Yeah, they were there!"

At 11:00, Nicole took the court against Lucy, whose family was in Wisconsin visiting relatives. She played competitive junior tennis in the Southwest section. Nicole was a bit nervous, since she knew nothing about her opponent. After the warm-up, Lucy, a second-year fourteen with solid strokes, told Nicole she hoped for a ranking this year. Lucy won the serve. Nicole chose to have the sun at her own back.

Lucy had a unique serve. She would hold the racquet over her back with her elbow high in the air as if she were scratching her back, then toss the ball with her left hand and bring her racquet arm up to make contact. With a ball-holder on her waist, she needed to hold only one ball at a time. These two different methods were quite foreign to Nicole. Nicole found herself wondering whether they were common place in the Southwest. Regardless, Lucy was very accurate with her serve, and her second serve was stronger than Nicole's.

The match was extremely competitive, moving to 3-3, each game very close. Lucy had a fine overall game and tried whenever possible to get to the net with an array of approach shots. She used under-spin to hit balls down the lines, or angled the ball deep and off the court, then approached the net. She jumped on weak returns; concluding with strong volleys and overheads. Nicole had never experienced playing anyone so eager to take chances to get to the net. Lucy seemed to live on the edge. To compensate, Nicole quickly realized she needed to return the ball deep as often as possible. When Lucy came to the net, Nicole made sure her passing shots were accurate and on occasion even utilized her lob.

The match became a battle of wills. It became a test for Nicole to combat a very aggressive opponent. The score was 5-5 before Lucy suffered her first double-fault. Nicole then decided to try something different. She hit a ball hard to Lucy's backhand deep in the corner; then followed the ball in. Now *she* was the aggressor. Lucy countered with a backhand lob, but the ball fell short and Nicole put it away with an overhead so hard that the ball bounced over the fencing. Embarrassed, Nicole offered, "Sorry—my fault."

When Nicole won six of the next seven points to take the first set, 7-5, Lucy changed her game. She became less aggressive and stood back on the baseline, where Nicole was the better player. Lucy charged the net only twice in the second set, and the match ended in a 7-5, 6-2 victory for Nicole.

Nicole sighed with relief as she met Lucy at the net.

"You get to the net really well, Lucy," Nicole complimented her opponent.

"My coach says that if I continue to play that way, my game will get better when I'm older. He said I could be a great serve-and-volley player."

Nicole smiled. "He's probably right Lucy. Great match!"

Now in the semis, Nicole went to confirm her next opponent, although she had a feeling she already knew who she'd be playing. As predicted, Erin won in straight sets, 6-0 and 6-0 'double donuts', over Jill Stanley of Sauk Prairie. Erin and Nicole would play each other at 2:00.

With the temperature starting to soar, the Harrises grabbed a quick lunch at the local Dog'N Suds. Jon wanted a root-beer float. Nicole wanted air-conditioning. The air felt good and Nicole made her customary change into a dry outfit. Nicole felt it was such a privilege to have extra clothes along. Gram's Christmas present turned out to be a real Godsend!

As they left the restaurant, Mia asked, "How did you know when to change your game and get more aggressive?"

"I remembered reading in a book last winter, when your opponent has the upper hand, change your game—even to the point of mimicking *their* game."

Mia thought about this for a moment and replied, "Nicole, how profound!"

At 1:45 Nicole and Erin were called to the desk, and sent to their court to warm up. Nicole served first to start the match. Both girls were extremely accurate from the baseline, not giving any ground. Each played with extreme focus and points averaged eight to ten returns each. Today, Nicole did not at all feel intimidated playing Erin. In fact, she felt quite comfortable playing Erin. Nicole wasn't sure if it was because she was used to Erin's playing style from practicing with her, or if Lucy had inbred in her the importance of accuracy from the baseline with *no* short balls. Regardless, Nicole held her own, and the score in the first set went to 4-4.

Nicole started game nine with a rare double fault. Then, adding insult to injury, followed with a short ball that Erin angled off the court for a winner. Erin attacked Nicole's next second serve with a beautiful approach shot that produced a weak return. Erin's volley to the corner secured the point. At 0–40, Nicole hit a rare ace towards the right middle of the box. The next point seemed to last forever, before Nicole hit the ball just wide right. Erin took the next game and the set, 6-4.

The second set was much like the first. Again Erin took the slight upper hand with her fine shot selection and beautiful form, to secure a 6-4 set win and match. It had been a great, high-level competition. With the loss, Nicole at best could finish third; and at worst finish in fourth place equivalent to her tournament seeding. Terry Williams beat Susan Minifie 6-4, 7-6, so at 10:00 tomorrow, Nicole was scheduled to match up with Susan in a duel for third place. Erin and Terry would play for the first place trophy. Erin and Nicole planned a 9:00 warm-up, said goodbye and headed to the parking lot. Nicole realized that it will be her last match before the all-important state closed, and hoped to finish tomorrow on a high note.

At 8:30 Sunday morning, Carol dropped Jon off at his friend Jimmy's house to spend the day, before driving Nicole and Mia back out to Waukesha, for the conclusion of the tournament. Erin was already there, and the girls warmed up. Erin told Nicole that she was not going to play with her usual doubles partner in the upcoming closed tournament and asked Nicole if she would like to play with her.

"Absolutely," said Nicole. "It was so much fun in Kohler."

The director called the players up. Nicole and Erin wished each other luck and planned to meet after the matches. Nicole introduced herself to Susan and together made their way to Court Two. Erin and Terry proceeded to Court One for the championship match. After a short warm-up, the girls got started. Susan, a very tall girl, liked to use her height at the net, a strategy Nicole quickly noted as they warmed up. Had it been a stroke of luck that she played Lucy in her first match? After all, didn't Mia always say, "Everything happens for a reason!"

Nicole won the spin and served first. Her main goal, she decided, was to keep her first-serve percentage high, to deny Susan quick access to the net. And, yes, the match grew eerily similar to Nicole's match with Lucy. Whenever possible, Susan rushed the net where she did great damage. Nicole found herself sprinting to her baseline position to arrive early and stepped into each shot. A larger girl, Susan did not have great speed, and Nicole moved her around the court, on occasion changing up and shortening her usually deep ball with an under-spin shot short across court. This let Susan rush the net, but off balance and not on her terms. Nicole was able to squeak out the first set in a nail-biter, 7-5.

Nicole knew that the match was far from over. Susan was very determined to take the second set and send the match to three sets. Consequently, Nicole recognized that she needed to step up her own performance. To regain control, Susan began to serve and volley. Fortunately, Nicole was able to block each ball and used the force of the serve to send the ball not only back, but deep into the court, compliments of practicing with Mr. Novak and overcoming his piercing serve. This forced Susan into much longer volleys than she intended. Often, the result was a short ball in Nicole's court; giving her a passing shot down the line. Nicole's ability to minimize the serve and volley and keeping her own first serve percentage high paid off. On the set's last point, Susan hit a sure winner to the corner, but Nicole rushed to return the ball and delivered a lob just over the on-rushing Susan. Susan stopped short, ran back almost to the back net, and lobbed the ball back weakly. Nicole quickly rushed in and caught the ball in the air before it had a chance to even bounce, and volleyed the ball to the opposite corner. It hit the line, giving her the set 6-3, match, and third place victory.

Nicole surprised herself with her shot selection, since she never attempted the shot, a swing volley, before today. Nicole ran to the net and congratulated Susan on a fine match.

Erin had been watching Nicole. As Nicole walked off the court, Erin greeted Nicole and gave her a hug. "Nicole, that was a big time shot. I don't even know if I would have tried it." Erin offered.

"Thanks, Erin. How did you do?"

"I won 6-2, 6-2."

"Great Job, Erin!"

The girls walked together to the desk to report the score. Nicole received the third-place trophy; Susan, the fourth. Nicole and Erin discussed the State Closed Tournament. Since there was only eight days before the tournament, they agreed to hit a few times in the coming week. The Harrises left for home.

Carol told Nicole, "You really played well. I was amazed at the level of your play in this tournament. Your hard work and practice really are paying off."

Gram added, "Nicole, you really rose to the occasion. I'm so proud of you!"

The following week was one of great anticipation. Everything Nicole had worked for would soon be on the line. Only the top four or five girls from the closed would be invited to the Western Sectional in East Lansing, Michigan. Nicole very much wanted to be one of them. When she mentioned the possibility of making it to the Westerns, Carol said, "Let's cross that bridge when we come to it!"

Nicole practiced with Erin twice during the week. During one of the practices, Mr. Nelson informed Nicole that the Wisconsin district of the Western Section had always been notoriously weak.

"The Wisconsin district has far fewer girls than Michigan, Illinois, and Indiana. We're lucky if one or two of the girls from Wisconsin are even seeded in the Sectional Tournament." Mr. Nelson shared.

He continued, "Last year, Erin wasn't seeded, but our first two girls were. Erin had a great tournament and finished fourteenth."

In between playing with Erin, Nicole also played a few times with Mr. Novak. At the end of the practice session Mr. Novak stated emphatically, "Nicole you're really playing very well. You are indeed ready for this challenge. Make the most of it. Make us all proud!"

Finally, Nicole practiced once more, on her own at the park. It was a busy week. As if tennis wasn't enough, Nicole also had two dance practices for her recital, which was to be held right after the tournament. Every year the recital had a special number, a father-daughter dance. In the past, when Nicole saw her dance classmates waltz across the stage with their dads, it had made her sad. At times like this, she missed her dad so much.

Carol put a great deal of thought into this dilemma and secretly called Mr. Novak. Carol informed him about the recital and before she could even ask him, he jumped in, "I would be very honored—if it's okay with Nic."

"Nicole told me about her recital," he said. "Besides, my wife told me my dancing needs a lot of work!" he added.

That night after dinner Carol pulled Nicole aside. "Nicole," she said, "What would you think about Mr. Novak dancing with you at the recital? I mentioned it to him and he seemed quite willing."

"He was?" Nicole asked. "Can I just think about it for a while?"

"Of course, Honey. It's completely up to you."

A few hours later, Nicole came out from her room. She

made her decision. She called Mr. Novak and formally asked him. He was excited and happy to participate, but informed Nicole that she would have to give him dance lessons as well. Nicole mentioned the two mandatory practice sessions. He confirmed that he could make them.

Saturday night before the church service, Nicole lit a special candle for Dad. She did this often, always the fourth candle from the left. Not only did they both love the number four, but the left side is closest to the heart. With the candle lit, she offered a short prayer, "Dad, I wish you could be the one to dance with me next week. I'm sorry you can't be. Mr. Novak is temporarily taking your place. I just wanted you to know. You will always be my Dad. I love you."

The prayer made Nicole feel more at ease. To Nicole, she now had her Dad's permission.

In the back of the church the Harrises bumped into Dr. Stanwood, his wife Rita, and little Jenny. Giving Nicole a big hug, Jenny asked Nicole when she was going to babysit for her again. Dr. Stanwood said that he had been hearing good things about Nicole at his club. While Nicole was embarrassed by his comment, he continued—"Move over, Chris Everett!" He asked Carol about the Collins baby at work and made sure that the Harris family was all set for their week at the lake in late August. Jon asked if they still had the canoe from last year. "It's sitting there waiting for you, Jon, as we speak," he replied. Everyone laughed.

That night Cindy came home with the Harrises and stayed for the night. They enjoyed grilled bratwurst and hot dogs. Mia made her famous German potato salad. They ate on the back patio, at the redwood table that Nicole's dad had made for the family. After dinner, everyone cleaned up. The sun had gone down behind the trees. It was starting to cool off.

For desert, they drove to Kopps in Glendale, the best custard in the North Shore area. The girls were excited. They had not been to Kopps since the all-star baseball game, which seemed so long ago. The girls looked forward to getting their cones and sitting out in the picnic area to chat. As they were choosing their spot, they spied the Stanwoods, who joined them. Then, coincidentally, Erin and her parents showed up—the first opportunity for the Harrises to meet Mrs. Nelson, in her early thirties and with a beautiful tan. Her clothes were trendy and her hair was stylishly frosted. She was very friendly and pleased to meet everyone. Everyone enjoyed each other's company. Mr. Nelson talked to Dr. Stanwood about tennis. Both played in the men's league at their clubs. Erin and Cindy had heard so much about each other, and finally had the opportunity to meet. Little Jenny remained glued to Nicole the entire time. It was a very pleasant, impromptu evening.

The next morning Cindy's mom picked her up after breakfast. They were going to pick up Cindy's aunt and get manicures. Cindy wished Nicole good luck in her big tournament. "I'll see you at recital practice on Friday night," said Nicole. "And by the way, Mr. Novak agreed to do the father-daughter dance with me."

"Awesome," replied Cindy. "That will be so-o-o much fun."

On Monday afternoon, Nicole snuck in one last practice with Mr. Novak at 3:45, right after work. Nicole showed up early and hit against the backboard. He arrived right on time, in a great mood and holding a box. He opened the box and showed Nicole a new pair of shiny black shoes his wife bought him for the recital.

"Wow, Mr. Novak! You're really stylin! Those are cool!"

"Now, if I can only dance in them!"

He put the shoes aside, and they began their regular stretching routine, which by now was commonplace. About a month ago, Mr. Novak told Nicole that he had played baseball in junior college. He remembered some stretches that provided a great warm-up to prevent injuries. Nicole liked the idea and as a result they agreed to incorporate them into their practice routine. Nicole also started to regularly stretch before her other sports activities. The stretching made her feel more limber and to date, had helped to prevent any sports related injuries.

They played for an hour and fifteen minutes, hitting the ball well, with some great points. Then Nicole worked on service returns and volleys. As they left the court, Mr. Novak told Nicole he had something for her. He opened the trunk of his car and handed her a card, indicating a year's subscription to *Tennis Monthly*. "Nicole, I thought this might be something you could use. And there's a good chance your picture will be in there someday."

"Wow! You didn't have to get me anything, Mr. Novak. Gosh, thanks a million!"

"The pleasure is all mine. Good luck tomorrow! I know you'll do just fine."

Nicole quickly walked the few blocks to her home thinking about tomorrow, her big day. Nicole's first match was scheduled for 10:00 at North Shore Country Club. Pensive, Nicole believed she had done everything within her power to prepare for the tournament. Now, she just needed a good night's sleep and to wake up refreshed.

# EMPLOY A SITTING POSITION

**M**ia woke Nicole at 7:30 in the morning with, "Rise and shine, it is *your* time." Nicole laughed. "Good morning, Grandma," she said.

Gram had a special breakfast of pancakes and sausages ready, which they all enjoyed. By the time they finished, Carol returned from work. They sat for fifteen minutes and relaxed.

"I saw Dr. Stanwood last night. He said to be sure to tell you good luck today. I'm going to your first match, but then I have to come home and get some rest for tonight."

"It sure seems like you are working a lot of hours lately, Mom."

"We have just been very busy. There must be a full moon!"

Nicole left the table to get ready. She dressed and did several of the stretching exercises that Mr. Novak showed her. By 8:45, Nicole was all set and ready to go. She asked her Mom if she could make two quick stops. First, she wanted to stop at the park and second, she requested to make a quick stop at church to light a candle.

"Sure honey," Carol replied.

Nicole spent only fifteen minutes at the park. She practiced strokes and a few second serves, just enough to break a sweat. At St. Elizabeth's she once again lit the fourth candle from the left.

She prayed silently, "Dear Jesus, all my angels and Dad, please be with me today and help me to play to the best of my ability. I am grateful for the opportunity that awaits me today. Amen."

Carol waited in a pew in the back of the church.

"Are you ready, Sweetie?" she asked.

"Yes, I think I am," answered Nicole.

They drove in silence to the North Shore Racquet Club, a short twenty-minute trip. Carol intuitively knew that Nicole was mentally preparing for the day ahead. It was only 9:20 in the morning, but since it was late June in Wisconsin, it was already humid and starting to heat up. Fortunately for all the players, North Shore had twelve beautiful indoor courts. All the matches were scheduled to be played indoors today. As they drove up, they realized that the parking lot was almost full. Nicole quickly noticed a familiar motor home.

"Mom, the Gunthermans are here already," she announced.

"Who are they?"

"Oh, never mind, Mom. It's not that important."

The main entrance to the lobby was already jammed with players and families. The few places to sit were long ago taken. Tennis bags and gear covered the floor; were dropped everywhere. Many people were sitting on the floor. Looking around, Nicole noticed only one other wooden racquet besides hers.

The atmosphere was serious, unlike anything Nicole had ever seen. Many people were scanning the *Tennis Bible*. Others were talking loudly and flaunting their travel plans to Michigan, even though the eligibility was still undetermined.

The main tournament desk and the posted draw were two deep in onlookers.

As her family waited in the corner, Nicole made her way to check in. Halfway through the crowd she bumped into Erin and her dad and exchanged greetings.

"They're just about ready to start," he said.

Nicole quickly checked in and hurried to her spot with her family. Right beside her was Heidi Miller. Nicole leaned over and asked. "How is your ankle doing?"

"Oh, it's completely healed. Thanks for asking!"

Over all the loud noise, the tournament director, Mrs. Lawrence, announced that match play was about to begin. As she convened the players at one end of the lobby, Nicole felt like she was in a sorority or club. She recognized so many of these girls from tournaments over the past month. However, the group did not seem to be very friendly. Most weren't even talking to each other. Several of the players Nicole had never seen before.

Mrs. Lawrence went over the rules of play and etiquette. She related a story about a match from a few years ago. "On one occasion, a player received a return from an opponent. It clearly appeared to be long, and she called it out before the ball hit the surface. Just before the ball actually struck, a strong wind blew the ball back in play. The player had made her call too early. Her call was in error. The moral of the story? Never make a call prematurely. Wait for the ball to hit, each and every time. You never know what's going to happen."

A few groans of disbelief sounded from the veteran players. Erin told Nicole that Mrs. Lawrence was a stickler for details. A few years back she officiated a charity-fundraiser match between Chris Everett and Martina Navartalova. During the match she called several close foot faults on Chris, making her very upset. Even Martina asked her to overlook them. The crowd 'booed' Mrs. Lawrence, but she wouldn't give an inch.

It was time to call the names for the 10:00 matches. As she waited, Nicole studied the draw. She saw thirty-one girls listed in the singles 14's—players from Madison, Wausau, La Crosse, Rhinelander, Dodgeville, Green Bay, Kenosha, Stephens Point, and locals from Milwaukee County.

Erin was listed as the top seed of the tournament. Nicole was pleasantly surprised to find herself seeded third. With this draw, it would require four matches for all the girls to get to the finals, except for Erin. She had a first-round bye.

Eight teams were listed in the girls' doubles 14's. The Smith twins, Lindsey and Megan, from Mequon, were the top seeds. Erin and Nicole were seeded second. The twins did not play many singles matches but rather concentrated on doubles. Their father had been a professional doubles player. Some say that the two are so unbelievable together that they must have been joined at the hip!

In the singles, the seeding was:

Singles

1. Erin Nelson - Glendale, WI
2. Terry Williams - Brookfield, WI

3.  Nicole Harris - Milwaukee, WI
4.  Susan Minifie - Waukesha, WI
5.  Sara Cummings – Elm Grove, WI
6.  Colleen Henderson – Hartland, WI
7.  Lindsey Smith - Mequon, WI
8.  Megan Smith - Mequon, WI

Nicole was scheduled to play Ann Guntherman, from Madison in the opening round. The two were called and Nicole introduced herself.

Ann asked, "Are you really from Milwaukee?"

"Yes," said Nicole.

"Do you live downtown?"

"No, not at all."

They began their warm-up. Ann, a petite girl, had good-looking strokes. Nicole noticed that Ann did not hit the ball very hard. Thinking ahead, Nicole realized that this would allow her to have ample time to set herself up for her shots. Ann used a Head racquet and had two others in her bag. She asked Nicole why she was not using graphite. Nicole replied, "I just feel comfortable using this one."

Ann won the spin and served first. Nicole, a bit nervous, just wanted to get the first point behind her. Nicole returned the serve deep and cross-court. This forced Ann to hit a short return that hit the service line. Nicole moved up quickly, set herself, and powered the ball, angling off the other side of the court for a winner. Immediately, her jitters were gone.

The points continued much the same. Ann would hit a short ball, and Nicole would exploit the shot. Nicole's first-serve percentage was very high, and she won the first set 6-0. Serving and up 4-1 in the second, Nicole hit an ace to the inside part of the service box, then followed with three more aces on first serves. Nicole couldn't believe how well she was hitting the ball. Although Ann made a come-back in the final game, Nicole finished the match with a backhand winner up the line.

The girls shook hands at the net.

"Nicole, nice match. You sure played well."

"Thanks Ann. You're a fine player. I had a good day."

The girls reported to the desk and met their families, who had watched the match from a window a court away. The girls received times for their next matches. With this victory, Nicole moved on through the main draw to the round of sixteen. Ann moved to the back-draw with a chance to finish fifth in the double-elimination tournament. At 2:00 Nicole would play Julie Knox from Green Bay, who won her first match 6-4, 6-2 over Pam Lewis. Since it was already 11:30, Nicole cleaned up and changed in the bathroom. The family decided to eat lunch at Kopps, only a few miles away.

On the way, Carol mentioned that she heard some people talking about birthdays and tennis.

"Nicole, did you know that according to tennis, you have a 'bad birthday'?"

"What does that mean?"

"The first-year fourteens include anyone whose birthday is in the same calendar year. A player with a January birthday is the same age as one with a December birthday, even though she is most likely a grade ahead in school. You are a first-year fourteen with a December birthday. That makes you one of the youngest players here at age twelve."

"In essence, a second-year fourteen could be almost two years older than a first-year fourteen at some point—possibly two grades apart," said Gram.

"Wow, that's incredible! I know that Erin is a second-year fourteen with a January birthday. She's in eighth grade and will be in high school next year. I never thought about that."

They had never been to Kopps over the lunch hour on a weekday. It was very crowded. As Carol parked, Nicole and Jon got in line. They collected their food and found a shady spot on the patio. The sun felt good. The indoor courts had been quite chilly; almost too cold.

"I am so surprised that the tournament is so formal. It is so different  than the other local tournaments that you played over the past month. It doesn't seem like very much fun. Are you having a good time, Nicole?" Carol asked her daughter.

"I'm having fun, but there is a lot of pressure, since you are all by yourself. But it's a great feeling when you figure out how to counter someone in a match and it works. I remember reading once, if you just play the *ball* and forget about *who* you are playing, it takes away some of the pressure."

"Well said, Nicole," Mia reinforced.

The tournament was running close to schedule, so Nicole had about an hour to wait. She noticed Erin in the corner, glancing around, ready to start at any moment. Nicole remembered Erin telling her, Phillip Sweeney, a cute boy from her tennis club, was going to come to watch her play. The two took lessons together, and were good friends. "I'll have to introduce you," she said.

Erin heard the call for her match.

"Good luck," Nicole said.

"Thanks Nicole. You, too!"

Nicole returned to sit with her family. Jon had a few quarters, so to pass the time, he and Nicole played Pac-Man, a family favorite. Jon was definitely the family's Pac-Man champion. The time went by quickly. About 1:45 Julie and Nicole got their call. The two picked up the balls from the tournament desk and made their way to the court. Carol wished Nicole luck and left to get some sleep. Julie, a Green Bay resident, was a tall girl. She moved from Tampa, Florida about six months ago. She didn't know anyone in the tournament. Nicole said, "I remember going through that last year."

As they warmed up, Nicole noticed that Julie was left-handed. Nicole had never played a southpaw before, and it seemed very different. Julie did not hit her backhand with topspin. Instead, she cut under the ball with one hand. Often this resulted in lower shots that would sit up. Nicole had no problem reaching them, but really had to bend to return them with topspin. Nicole's returning a few under-spin shots with backspin herself, seemed to make it easier and gave her more confidence.

Julie won the racquet spin and served first. Her solid first serve and second serve with ample spin gave her good control. Her game plan seemed to consist of hitting under-spin approach shots deep to the corners and following them in, hoping to reach the service line for controlled volleys. Though her under-spin shots were slow, they were deep and afforded her time to sneak into position. Before long Nicole realized, hitting under-spin returns gave Julie more time to react and to make superior volleys. Methodically and intentionally, Nicole started to hit topspin to keep the ball deep.

It soon became a battle of wills. Every once in a while, with Julie deep on the baseline, Nicole would hit a drop shot just over the net to keep Julie off balance. Most of the games were close; however Julie won a few, decisively. With unique game and set scoring, tennis is a game where you can win a set scoring fewer points than your opponent. This *was* the case. Nicole felt fortunate to claim the first set 6-4. She played fine tennis and yet Julie was right on her heels.

The next set began with both girls playing solid tennis. Julie gave Nicole every indication that the match was a long way from being over. Nicole's serve was improving and she began the first game with two aces. In response, Julie rushed the net and hit a crushing volley for a winner. With Julie up at the net again on the following point, Nicole delivered a perfect topspin lob to the corner. Julie pursued the ball, but was left with no return. Nicole followed with a penetrating serve that pulled Julie off the court, then followed her serve in, expecting a weak return. Sure enough, the ball sailed short, and glided just over the net; affording Nicole the opportunity to smash a volley to the corner, taking game one.

For the rest of the set, Nicole mixed up her game to keep Julie off balance. The games were close, but the difference was Nicole's overall game and her uncanny ability to counter Julie's strategy with changes that denied Julie her comfort zone. Nicole won the second set, 6-4.

Day One was now in the books. Jon and Mia greeted Nicole with happy hugs. With this win, Nicole advanced to the round of eight. If she won again, she would be in the final four and could earn a spot to play in Michigan at the sectionals. At the desk, Mrs. Lawrence announced to the crowd that there would be at least five spots going to the sectional, but most likely not a sixth.

Erin won her first match 6-0, 6-0 and waited for Nicole to finish her match. The two girls hugged, and congratulated each other before checking the draw. Erin was to play the eighth seed, Megan Smith at 9:00. Nicole's next opponent was Heidi Miller, also scheduled to start at 9:00. Heidi upset the sixth seed, Colleen Henderson, in three sets, 4-6, 6-4, and 6-3. Obviously, Heidi's ankle must be better!

Tomorrow would be a big day. Nicole knew she had to be ready. The Harrises bid goodbye to Mrs. Lawrence and Erin and headed home. Nicole called Mr. Novak to give him an update as promised. He was not yet home from work, so Nicole talked to his wife, Peggi, who was very excited to hear the news. She promised to relay the great news, and wished Nicole luck for tomorrow's matches.

Nicole showered and got ready for supper. Mia was cooking tonight since Carol was still sleeping. It was great that Mom spent the morning at the tournament, but she really needed more sleep since she was scheduled to work again tonight at 11:00. Consequently, she would not be able to attend tomorrow's match. Nicole left her a little note about her match. With some coaxing from Gram, Nicole retired a little earlier than usual. Too much had been invested to not take necessary precautions. Besides, Mia knew Nicole well enough and understood that the day had been very draining, mentally and physically.

Nicole woke up early. It was only 6:30. She knew that she didn't need to get up for at least another hour, so she just laid in bed thinking about the day ahead. She made great progress this year, but wondered if it would be enough to get her to Michigan. Most likely, she would know by the end of the day today. She pictured herself in Michigan, competing for a chance to go to the famed national tournament, and smiled as those delightful thoughts swept through her mind. Would the family be able to afford the trip to Michigan if she earned a spot? Nicole decided to think about first things first. This meant focusing her efforts on what she could control; playing solid tennis and doing her best to win today. She hoped it would be enough.

She reached for her magazine on the nightstand and thumbed through it. An article featured Jennifer Capriati. She, too, had come far at a young age. Product of a famed tennis academy in Florida, she was now a superstar, a genuine teen idol. It all seemed so glamorous but so far, far away. Nicole loved her life. Yes, win or lose, she knew her family would always be there for support. Even if handed a golden opportunity, she could never leave her family for tennis. Simply, the two were so entwined.

A knock came at the bedroom door.

"Morning, Nicole. Rise and shine."

"Hi, Mia. I'm already awake. I'll be right out."

# 7

# GRIP IT ... AND RIP IT!

T he sun shone beautifully as they ate breakfast. Mia's oatmeal tasted so good.

Jon was going to spend the day at Jimmy's house, so today it would be just Gram and Nicole. After breakfast and Nicole's stretching, the two made a quick stop at the park and then went to St. Elizabeth's. There Nicole lit her particular candle and prayed for her special intentions for the day. Afterwards, she felt ready to take on the world.

At 8:30, there were far fewer cars in the club parking lot, since several players had been eliminated on Day One. Nicole saw Erin practicing on the first court with her dad. Erin spotted Nicole at the same time and the two girls quickly warmed up together for about ten minutes before their call. They wished each other good luck, and agreed to meet right after the matches.

"Good morning, Heidi," Nicole said as she approached the desk.

"Hi, Nicole," said Mrs. Lawrence. "You girls will be on Court Four." She handed the balls to Nicole—Penn fours, Nicole noticed. "Good luck, ladies."

As the two girls warmed up, Nicole hoped that this is a sign. Could Court Four and the number four balls be a mere coincidence? Heidi was moving and hitting the ball well, with no sign of her ankle injury. Nicole knew it will be a tough match. Heidi felt she should have won the Janesville tournament. She intended to prove why she had been the top seed in that tournament. It was only fair that she play Heidi at her full strength.

At the net, Nicole spun her racquet, and opted to serve first. Nicole lined up, took a deep breath, and adjusted her headband. Her serve was returned across the court and deep. Nicole ran, set her feet, but swung a little late. The ball sailed over the net to the middle of the court, where Heidi smacked an inside-out forehand to the deep corner on Nicole's backhand side. Nicole ran down the ball, but could hardly get racquet on it; 0-15. On the next point, Heidi sent a forehand winner down the line. It was evident she had great confidence in her forehand, and had yet to hit one backhand. When Nicole missed a first serve, Heidi jumped on the second for a cross-court forehand winner; 0-40. With Heidi standing deep, Nicole resorted to her second serve on her first offering. Heidi ran up, but angled the ball off the court. Nicole's next serve was solid, yet Heidi returned it well. Nicole was able to hit the ball to Heidi's backhand. She returned the ball with far less power, leaving it short. Nicole ran up but hit the ball off the court—an unforced error.

Heidi won the first game. Even though she was down, Nicole was hopeful that she could play with Heidi. Nicole planned to exploit Heidi's backhand, to hit the ball cross-court to her backhand whenever possible. If she had to hit to her forehand, she intended to play the ball hard and deep or keep it short with under-spin. She was determined to minimize Heidi's opportunity to use her powerful forehand.

Nicole returned Heidi's first serve sharply down the line. Heidi ran to the ball, but had to hit a backhand return, short. Nicole ran up, and this time hit a drop shot that barely cleared the net. Heidi ran up, but couldn't get a racquet on the ball. Nicole returned Heidi's next serve deep, to the middle of the court. Heidi hit a forehand crosscourt to Nicole's forehand. Nicole hustled over. With Heidi deep on the baseline, she hit a short under-spin shot cross-court about five feet past the net. Heidi raced in, but used under-spin which left her return short. Anticipating a short return, Nicole was ready with a backhand topspin lob over Heidi to the corner. The battle continued throughout the entire first set, with Nicole exploiting Heidi's backhand and Heidi doing all she could to use her powerful weapon. In the see-saw contest, Nicole barely took the first set, 6-4.

In the second set Nicole continued her deep, penetrating shots to Heidi's backhand and short balls to her forehand. On occasion Nicole erred and set Heidi up for her forehand, but Nicole's shot placement made a huge difference. Nicole prevailed; 6-3.

It had been a tough match. Never before, had Nicole ever had to continually think about ball placement as much. The girls congratulated each other with a handshake at the net and made their way to the desk. Nicole breathed a sigh of relief. She was now in the final four and had just punched her ticket to Michigan. Mia gave Nicole a big hug, as did Erin, who just defeated Megan Smith, 6-2, 6-2. By now, it was nearly 11:00. Erin asked Nicole to go to lunch with her and her dad, who insisted on treating. Mia decided this was fine, after Nicole changed into dry clothes. Mia opted to go home for several hours to do some housework, since both of the girls were next scheduled to play at 2:00.

After lunch at Thill Bros. in Bayshore, the girls returned, with an hour and a half to wait. All the top four seeds had prevailed. Nicole would once again face Terry Williams, the two seed. Erin would play Susan Minifie, the four seed. Erin asked her dad if she and Nicole could go next door to McDonald's. He agreed. He had to leave anyway for a meeting, and Erin's mom wasn't scheduled to arrive before 1:30, to take his place.

At McDonald's, Erin and Nicole talked and played amid the piles of balls, and made their way through all the tunnels, slides and ladders, laughing all the while. They redid each other's hair, talked about the boys at school. They had a great time; both looking conspicuously out of place especially in light of the pressure each was under. They lost track of time and before they knew it, the time was 1:45. They quickly made their way back to the club. They arrived late with their crazy hairstyles and ran into Mia and a visibly upset Mrs. Nelson. Mrs. Nelson pulled Erin aside and told her to change her hair and get ready. Mia, on the other hand told Nicole their hairstyles were "very beauty salon creative." Nicole felt bad for Erin, so she re-combed her hair into a ponytail and put on her headband.

The semi-final matches were called. As Nicole was ready to take the court, Carol arrived. She had been lying in bed thinking about the match. She couldn't sleep. She congratulated Nicole on her victory, wished her good luck, and gave her a kiss and a hug. Nicole was happy her Mom came, but she couldn't help but wonder if her Mom realized that she was eligible to play in the Western sectional?

As Nicole took the court, she recalled her first match with Terry two months ago. Nicole knew she came a long way since then, but so had everyone else. There was talk in the club that if Terry and Erin prevailed, each would be seated at the Westerns. Terry was a good, very smart, all-around player. Nicole knew this. Nicole had played Erin twice and had improved considerably. When they last met, Terry had exploited Nicole's second serve and had worked her way to the net for volleys, often resulting in winners. So much of tennis was keeping the ball deep against the opponent. This was once again, Nicole's major objective.

Terry and Nicole's warm-up was very spirited. Terry won the racquet spin and chose to serve first. 'Deep, deep, deep,' thought Nicole as she readied herself for her shots. Terry started the match with a serve wide right. Her second attempt Nicole sent deep and across the court. Terry sent it back cross-court to Nicole. With what appeared to be a slight opening, Nicole pointed her left foot and aimed the ball down the line with topspin. The shot was deep, and Terry scurried to retrieve it. She backhanded the ball on the run, for a short return. Nicole hustled in and put the ball away for a winner.

It was exactly what Terry had done to Nicole in the first meeting. Nicole was pumped. The game became a battle of wills. Both girls quickly moved in and out, back and forth, all over the court to return every ball deep and refused to give in. Some points lasted more than twenty strokes. Soon a crowd gathered above, to watch the entertaining match. Nicole continued to get her first serve in. Terry was able to take advantage of her second serve only twice. The end of the first set was neck and neck, 6-6, a tiebreaker. Whoever scored seven points first by a margin of two or more would claim the set. The players would alternate serves on odd points. After six points, the players switched sides. This was Nicole's first tiebreaker. She would receive serve. She heard that it was tough to prevail if you fell behind in a tiebreaker. She was determined to be on top of her game.

Terry's first serve, a boomer, pulled Nicole off the court, and she did all she could to just hit a lame duck back over the net. Terry came up fast, took the ball right out of the air, and smacked it to the far corner for a winner. It was Nicole's opportunity to serve. Her first serve was long. As Terry edged slightly forward on the court, Nicole hit her second. Terry returned the ball short to the other side of the court, with under-spin. Nicole quickly moved up, but hit the ball into the net. Nicole was down; 2-0. Next, Nicole served solidly; Terry returned it long.

Amid a series of baseline shots, Terry and Nicole traded the next six points. Remarkably, in each instance, a short ball led to the player's demise. Behind 5-4, Nicole double-faulted for the first time. Terry was now at set point. Nicole missed with her next serve, but the second was good. Terry returned, and the girls each dug in on the baseline. After about fifteen hits, Terry's forehand hit the net and lamely fell over on Nicole's side. Terry won the tiebreaker, 7-4, and the first set, 7-6.

Nicole was very disappointed. She worked very hard; yet lost the set. The next set started out similarly; each player trying to keep the other deep. Terry took a 4-2 lead. Then Nicole stormed back to tie the set, 5-5. Terry won the next game, and went up 40-30; with match point. Again a lengthy rally occurred, until Terry's forehand caught the net and fell harmlessly on Nicole's side; point, set, match.

The girls met at the net to shake hands.

"Boy, have you improved since the last time we played!" Terry complimented Nicole.

"Thanks, Terry," replied Nicole, adding "You really played a nice match."

They walked off the court to report the score.

Carol and Mia told Nicole she had played fabulously. Erin told Nicole she played very tough. Nicole, the only first-year fourteen in the top four, would play for third place against Susan Minifie, whom Erin had defeated 6-1, 6-2. Erin and Terry would play for the championship at the same time, 9:00 a.m. Erin and Nicole would play their first doubles match in about an hour.

The two girls rested and refreshed themselves for about forty-five minutes. For their doubles match, they would face Samantha Andrews and Ann Guntherman both from Madison. This was the first doubles match the girls would play together. After all the pressure of the singles, the doubles match seemed like a walk in the park. Erin and Nicole had far better strokes and far more experience. The match ended in only forty minutes, in a 6-0, 6-0 victory. Erin and Nicole were now in the doubles semi-finals, slated to start after the singles play tomorrow.

It had been a long day at the club. Carol, Mia, and Nicole slowly made their way to the car. Tomorrow was the final day of the tournament. Nicole was a bit down, re-living the close match with Terry.

Mia offered, "Nicole, I can't believe how well you played Terry. She is a great player.

The difference between this match and the one at Lake Country is night and day. We are so proud of you."

After Nicole offered her thanks, Carol added, "Nicole, I have a little something for you." as she handed Nicole an envelope.

"What is this, Mom?"

"Open it up. Look inside."

Nicole opened the envelope. "I see that it's from the American Automobile Association, but I'm not sure what it is. What's the long highlighted line on each page?"

"It's a Trip-Tik. If you follow the line from page one to the end, it will take you from our house all the way to East Lansing, Michigan."

Nicole screamed. "Oh my gosh, we can *go*?"

"Absolutely. You've earned it. I've been working extra hours. Dr. Stanwood was kind enough to give me this Trip-Tik. We love you, honey. I even got the week off from work."

"Thanks, Mom!"

Once home, Nicole called Mr. Novak, who grew excited at the news. She reminded him about the recital practice tomorrow night. "How could I possibly forget?" he said. "I have to break in my new shoes!"

Then Nicole jumped into the shower, and slipped into her pajamas. For the rest of the night she planned to relax— and, of course, think about tomorrow. When Jon got home, the family sat down for Mia's famous spaghetti. Carol was off for the night, so everyone retired early for a solid night's sleep.

By 7:45, after a quick breakfast, the family was out the door. After a stop at the park and church, they arrived at the club. Erin and her dad were practicing on Court One. Erin and Nicole hit together for about fifteen minutes and finished with some serves. Mrs. Lawrence announced the two matches for first and third place.

It was time for Nicole to take the court for her last singles match at the Closed, and she was determined to go out strong. She wished Terry and Erin good luck and made her way to her court. After a quick warm-up, she and Susan were ready to begin. Nicole remembered her previous third-place match with Susan; her serve-and-volley game. Again she reminded herself, it would be imperative to return serves well and not concede short balls.

Susan served  first, and Nicole intended  to be the aggressor from the start. She rocketed the serve right back at Susan's feet. Susan had no time to react as the ball hit her leg and bounced off the court. Nicole's outstanding service returns denied Susan's serve-and-volley game through the entire set. She reached the net only once—when she hit a piercing shot forcing Nicole to return a short ball. Nicole played some of her best tennis and took the first set 6-2.

As the match continued, Nicole's first-serve percentage skyrocketed, as did her confidence. She started to string points together more consistently and took a commanding lead of 5-1. Mr. Nelson remarked to onlookers that Nicole's hustle and heart more than her strokes had validated her play. Nicole's play was near flawless as she made her way to the net on the final point, hitting a powerful forehand down the line and following it in. Susan ran to the ball, hit a cross-court shot on the run, and Nicole replied with a backhand volley deep to the opposite corner for a winner.

The match was over. As if by a miracle, Nicole finished third in the tournament. She met Susan at the net and congratulated her. Susan merely nodded. As the two entered the lobby, everyone broke into applause. Jon ran up and told Nicole that she was awesome. Carol and Mia gave her big hugs. Nicole, her cheeks still flushed from her effort, was all smiles.

"How is Erin doing?" Nicole asked as she excused herself and went to watch and cheer on her friend.

"Not that great right now," said Mr. Nelson. "She had a good start, 6-1, but now she's playing sluggishly and it's 4-4 in the second. She looks tired."

Erin glanced up, saw Nicole, and smiled. She took a deep sigh, then rallied to finish the set strongly, winning the last two close games.

"Thanks for coming over, Nicole. You must have inspired her," said Mr. Nelson.

"No, she's just a great player," said Nicole.

Mrs. Lawrence presented the trophies to all four girls, to enthusiastic applause. Earlier, she presented the fifth-place trophy to Sara Cummings. It was 10:30. The doubles semis were scheduled to start in an hour. The Smith twins and their opponents were scheduled to play the one match; while Erin and Nicole would face Sara Cummings and Colleen Henderson in the other. The girls grabbed an Orangina and rested in the lobby.

The hour passed quickly. The two doubles matches were on adjacent courts, One and Two. During the warm-up Nicole peeked over to see the Smith girls going through their routine. Both had very light blonde hair. Both were very beautiful.

Nicole and Erin won the racquet spin.　Erin would serve first. After Kohler, she and Nicole had worked on hand signals and felt more comfortable with one another. Erin's dad had given them some pointers a few weeks ago that added to their teamwork. Though solid players, Sara and Colleen lacked doubles experience. Several times during the match they found themselves out of place on the court, which cost them points. By game three of the second set, the other match had already ended, with the Smith girls winning 6-0, 6-0. Erin and Nicole's match was far more competitive, with some great points, but Erin and Nicole proved to be just too tough, winning 6-2, 6-2.

The final was scheduled for 3:00. Erin and her family left to go to lunch at Bay Shore. Nicole changed her outfit and went with her family once again to Kopps for lunch.

At 2:45 everyone was back on site. Nicole huddled with Erin and her father for last-minute pointers. The Smith girls consulted with their dad Mark, a very tall, lean man who had once been on the pro-circuit in doubles. Several times during the week Nicole had heard the Smith girls referred to as the "The Blonde Bombshells," and the two certainly fit the bill.

Shortly before 3:00, Mrs. Lawrence called the teams together. "This is the battle between the blondes and the brunettes," she smiled. "Best of luck to both teams. Have a great match."

The four girls made their way to the court for the warm-up. Nicole noticed that the Smith sisters didn't seem to hit the ball with power, but had fine form and terrific volleys. They had only lost one game in the tournament. Erin said they had finished fifth in the Western doubles last year and eighteenth nationally. Erin and Nicole needed to play well, if they hoped to win.

Lindsey and Megan won the spin and served first. Erin received serve, leaving Nicole in position up at the net. The match started out close; each team feeling the other out. Both teams held serve and stood locked, 3-3. In game seven the Smiths turned more aggressive. They served and volleyed, leaving both of them at the net. On occasion, as Nicole and Erin switched, the Smith up at the net poached and ran over to other side of the court for a quick, unexpected point. With calls coming from the player behind as if directing traffic, they switched positions periodically. They aimed to push Erin and Nicole back. Aggressively they advanced to get them away from the net.

The shifts in the Smiths' formation opened up the court. Several times Nicole and Erin found themselves out of position, and their opponents hit the ball between them or angled it off the court with crisp volleys. The consistent play of the Smiths was like that of a well-oiled machine. The court seemed to be much wider on Erin and Nicole's side than on the other.

Erin and Nicole continued to fight, although more often than not, seemed to be reacting to the aggressive play of the Smith girls. Several times all four girls found themselves at the net amid exciting multiple volleys. The crowd eagerly applauded. The Smiths won the first set 6-3. Up 5-3 in the second, Lindsey served at 40-30, match point. Erin made a great shot. Megan poached and missed the return. As Lindsey ran the ball down, Megan retreated. With both Smiths deep, Erin charged the net. She and Nicole were up, both Smith girls back. On the return, Lindsey hit a perfect topspin lob over Erin, and yelled "Go!" Both Smiths ran to the net. Erin got around the ball, but could only make a weak return, as Megan readied for an overhead. She smacked the ball for a 6-3, 6-3 victory.

The girls congratulated each other. The Smiths really impressed Nicole. Quickly she learned that doubles strategy was different—perhaps more sophisticated than that of singles. The four girls entered the lobby to broad applause, and received their trophies. As everyone was leaving, Nicole sought out Mrs. Lawrence and thanked her for hosting the tournament.

"You are certainly welcome, young lady," she replied. "And good luck in Michigan."

It had been an awesome week, a week Nicole could be proud of. As the Harris family departed, each wondered what would be next. At home, Nicole cleaned up and grabbed a bite to eat. In less than an hour Mr. Novak would arrive to pick her up for dance-recital practice.

Precisely at 6:00, the doorbell rang.

"Well, let's hear it! Tell me everything. What's the big news today?" Mr. Novak inquired as he quickly stepped inside.

Nicole told him she finished third in the tournament and second in the doubles.

"I qualified for Michigan, for the Western Sectional. Mom said we can go, can you believe it? I'm so excited!"

"Nicole, I am very proud of you. You have come so far! Congratulations. Mrs. Harris, you have a really hard worker for a daughter."

As Nicole and Mr. Novak were leaving, Carol added, "I'll see you in a few hours. *Don't* break a leg!"

# BE OUT IN FRONT

The big night of the recital finally arrived. Carol, Mia, and Jon arrived more than an hour early to secure good seats for themselves and Mrs. Novak. Twenty minutes later the Novaks came. By 6:00, the auditorium was filled with families and friends eagerly awaiting the performances. The excitement was palpable! Backstage it was equally electric, with more than one hundred kids preparing and lining up in their designated places. Mr. Novak and Cindy's dad said goodbye to the girls and left to take their seats in the audience to watch the show. The men were instructed to meet backstage shortly before the finale. At the end of the last recital practice, Nicole and Mr. Novak jokingly decided they were ready and up to the challenge to perform their special dance. They picked up the routine easily and Mrs. Kate positioned them front and center for the majority of the last dance. They felt proud of their accomplishment. "Bring it on!" they declared.

At 7:00 sharp the recital began. The music started; the curtain rose. From one side of the stage Mrs. Kate could be seen holding a clipboard and providing direction. Nicole's class performed two dances, both equally entertaining. The first was a snappy jazz number and the second a graceful ballet performed *en pointe*. Each demonstrated the skills developed and refined over the past year. As each dance concluded, the audience acknowledged the hard work of every dancer with generous applause.

The recital was an eclectic collection of dances, representing a wide range of class experience, from preschool through high school dance students. The night flew by. Before long, it was time for the eagerly awaited final dance routine. All the dads made a quiet exit to join their daughters backstage. Anticipation was building. Mr. Novak and Cindy's dad met in the aisle, and gave each other a high-five, ascended the stairs, and disappeared. As the curtain closed after the last number, the murmurs and chatter increased. The audience excitedly awaited the evening's final performance, the father-daughter dance. From behind the curtain, soft shuffling sounds could be heard. Occasionally the curtain even flapped open, prompting snickers from the crowd.

The curtain opened to reveal the fathers posed like statues beside their daughters. Kermit the Frog sang, "Someday we'll find it—the Rainbow Connection. The lovers, the dreamers, and me." The crowd roared with delight. The couples moved back and forth to the music, each rotating toward the front row to display its talents—or lack thereof. Even dads with two left feet didn't seem to care, and enjoyed their few minutes of fame onstage with their daughters. Nicole and Mr. Novak smiled amid their moment of glory. Feeling the music, Mr. Novak kicked his leg just a bit higher than most.

"How come John Travolta never dances with me that way?" Mrs. Novak asked to broad laughter.

The dance ended to thunderous applause rewarded with an encore. The second number was even funnier. At one point all the dads turned around at the same time and 'shook their booties' at the audience—to a standing ovation. The recital ended with a Grande Finale, as each class took their bows center stage.

The Harrises, Novaks, and Penns decided to celebrate at their favorite Italian restaurant. Mama Mia's was more crowded than usual. Everyone was grateful that Gram had thought ahead and made a reservation last week. After a short five minute wait, the Hostess called the Harris party. They all enjoyed a scrumptious meal of famous antipasto and assorted thin-crust pizzas. Witty references to the men's dancing enlivened the conversation; prompting Mr. Novak to re-think his decision to retire his dancing shoes.

Volleyball camp started the following week at nearby Brown Deer High School. When flyers went out in the spring to all the local elementary schools, Nicole and several of her volleyball teammates decided to hone their skills. The week-long camp met every day from 8 a.m. until 1 p.m., with a half-hour break at 10:30. Mrs. Lewis, a very seasoned, successful coach, made the camp fun and enjoyable. The girls built upon their volleyball fundamentals and learned some great new techniques. Everyone really liked receiving the official "Bump, Set, Spike Volleyball Camp 1989" T-shirt, with "GO FALCONS" proudly displayed on the back.

Cindy and Nicole were glad the camp was well attended. This afforded them the opportunity to participate in some challenging matches. Throughout the week, the girls were divided into different teams for short, very competitive matches. Cindy and Nicole especially enjoyed the matches they played as teammates. One match, all six girls from St. Elizabeth's played together. "This is great practice for our fall volleyball team," Cindy shouted to Nicole.

The week passed quickly. Friday afternoon, just after camp ended, Nicole once again picked up her racquet. The Westerns were only eighteen days away. Nicole started practicing with a vengeance, hitting against the wall for more than an hour. Tomorrow she and Mr. Novak scheduled time to play together. Nicole's whole focus and mindset shifted to tennis, tennis, and more tennis.

Fourth of July was always one of the Harrises' favorite holidays. They enjoyed watching the exciting Brown Deer parade of vehicles, music, and floats. For all the children, the highlight of the parade was scrambling for candy tossed by generous handfuls to the crowd.

This year was different. The few days prior, Jon had been quite sick with a stomach virus. On the 4th of July, Nicole started complaining of a queasy stomach as well. Carol checked Jon's temperature. He was running a fever.

"I'm sorry, honey, but you can't go to the parade this year!" Carol told Jon.

"If he can't go, I won't go either!" Nicole declared. "Besides, the downtown Milwaukee parade will be on TV. We can all watch it together."

Mr. Novak called later in the day.

"My wife and I were looking for you at the parade," he said.

Nicole told him that Jon was sick and they decided to

stay home. The next morning Mr. Novak called to see how Jon and Nicole were doing.

"Jon's temperature is down. He's feeling much better. Nicole too." Carol said. She ended her chat with a big smile. "That would be great!" she replied.

Once off the phone, Carol asked Jon and Nicole to grab some bags and go outside to help her clean up the yard. As they were about to start their cleanup, a car drove slowly down the street, all decorated in crepe paper. The driver, dressed as a clown, loudly beeped the horn. As he passed the house, he tossed an assortment of candy out the sunroof towards the children. Nicole and Jon gathered up the goodies. It was Mr. Novak's car, Nicole noticed. After three trips up and down the street, he stopped, parked, and got out.

"How did you like your private parade?" he asked.

The Harrises laughed and thanked him for improvising the 4th of July tradition.

The following day Nicole intended to practice with Erin. Early that morning, however, Erin's mom called.

"Erin's not feeling well, and won't be able to practice today," she said.

"Jon's been sick the last few days. Nicole will understand," Carol replied.

Nicole took the news in stride. She spent the next few hours at the park, working on her strokes. She hit forehand and backhand groundstrokes against the backstop. Then she hit volleys, and finally worked on her serve.

The next two days she played with Mr. Novak.

"Nicole, taking a little time off from tennis for your dance recital and volleyball camp, certainly didn't hurt your game!" Mr. Novak shared his observation with Nicole.

"Thanks, Mr. Novak." Nicole replied.

The next weekend was the annual summer church festival, complete with rides, games, a band, and great food. Gram helped out by husking corn and Carol once again called bingo numbers, just like the previous year. The festival was crowded and very successful. The kids loved the rides.

By far the lines for the Ferris wheel were the longest. When Nicole's turn came, she found herself paired with Thomas, a boy in her class. Thomas' friends laughed and could be overhead making 'smooch sounds' and yelled, "Ohhh, Thomas! Ooooo, Thomas and Nicole!"

They knew Thomas had a secret crush on Nicole.

"Boy, I hope we get stuck at the top—that would be cool!" he told Nicole as the Ferris Wheel rose into the air.

As the ride neared the top, Thomas got his wish. Thomas started glancing around nervously. Nicole had never seen him so out of control and tried to calm him. Looking somewhat pale, he asked, "Do you think we'll be okay?"

"Of course! Don't be such a doubting Thomas," replied Nicole.

They started to laugh, and enjoyed the ride.

The festival's chicken dinner was truly "finger-licking good." The corn that Mia spent the afternoon husking was sweet and tasty. Mr. Novak, who volunteered as a security person, spent much time in the beer tent, claiming it was part of his job. In the Bingo tent Carol could be heard shouting "B-4!" Mia quickly shouted "Bingo!"

Mr. Penn laughed and shouted across the table to Mia "Hey—an inside job?"

Mia was very happy to win twenty dollars for that round of Bingo. It made her day.

Now, with only eight days before the Michigan trip, Nicole started to practice extra hard. She met only once with Erin, but as usual had a lot of fun. Erin was feeling better and practicing with Jeff, her tennis pro, who came to her house for ninety minutes of drills and lessons every day. Erin was hitting the ball well, but was looking very thin. Meanwhile, Nicole continued to work against the board at the park, and played with Mr. Novak.

The day before the family was scheduled to leave for East Lansing, Nicole made a list of everything the family needed to take, to make sure nothing would be left behind. Mr. And Mrs. Novak and the Stanwoods sent Nicole cards, wishing her good luck in the tournament. Nicole called Cindy to say good-bye. Carrie came over to bid farewell. Erin and her dad were also leaving tomorrow, but they were flying to Michigan. Nicole and Erin had made plans to practice together in Michigan, late in the day. Nicole and Carol made a quick stop at church. Nicole lit her favorite candle, the fourth from the left. She prayed for guidance, for a safe trip, and most importantly to play up to her potential. By evening's end, the Harrises were packed and ready. Mom encouraged everyone to get a good night's sleep, since they intended to leave early, no later than 6:00 in the morning.

At 5:30 a.m. the alarm clock went off. Mia, up first, was ready to go. After their morning routines they packed the 1982 Chevy Nova. Jon brought several games along to help everyone pass the time. At 6:00 a.m., right on schedule, they left, Carol and Nicole in the front, Jon and Mia in the back. As navigator, Nicole followed the Trip-Tik that Dr. Stanwood obtained from AAA. Nicole used the map to find the best places to stop for gas. They drove a little more than two hours through the greater Chicago area, before stopping for breakfast.

The traffic was light and fast-moving. They made it all the way to Chesterton, Indiana, before Jon and Nicole realized that this was their first full-fledged trip outside Wisconsin. They didn't count their trip two years ago to Great America in Gurnee, Illinois, just across the Wisconsin border.

Breakfast time came. It felt good to stop and stretch. They were hungry, and the Denny's window ad for the Grand Slam beckoned them. They headed in and ducked into the restrooms. As they waited, the cool air felt good. The smell of bacon hung in the air. The waitress asked Nicole and Jon their ages, and gave them each a Kids' menu.

"But Nicole—aren't you playing in a fourteen's tournament?" Carol chuckled.

Mia laughed. "Don't forget—the little lady has a 'Bad Birthday'!"

They enjoyed the irony of playing in a Girls 14 tournament while legitimately enjoying selections from a Kids' twelve and under menu. The breakfasts were scrumptious. In only minutes, everyone became an official member of the "Clean Plate Club."

"Let's play twenty questions!" suggested Mia. Back on the road now, they enjoyed several rounds. Then Mia switched tactics to a mini-Spelling Bee challenging Nicole and Jon. The words increased in difficulty. When Nicole misspelled her word, Mia gave Jon an easy word to insure he would win. His correct spelling of "positive" made him the official winner of Mia's Spelling Bee Challenge.

The mental distractions made the time pass by quickly. As they noticed a "Welcome to Battle Creek" sign, everyone agreed it was time for lunch.

"Who knows what Battle Creek is known for?" asked Carol.

"I don't know," said Nicole.

"I have no idea," added Jon.

Carol gave a clue. "What do you like to eat for breakfast on mornings when Gram doesn't make her famous pancakes?"

"Cereal!" announced Jon.

"That's right! Battle Creek is famous because this is where the Kellogg Company is located. They call this place Cereal City."

Mia jumped in. "They make a lot of your favorite breakfast cereals right in this city," she added.

They stopped at McDonald's and Jon played in the kids' area for about fifteen minutes. Nicole joined him, and the two could be heard laughing and enjoying themselves. It had been just a few weeks since she had done the same with Erin. After lunch, they stopped at a gas station to fuel the car for the final leg. Next stop? East Lansing, Michigan, home of Michigan State University. The tournament was to be held at a local high school.

As they neared Lansing, they spotted many signs advertising hotels and motels. It didn't take long for Jon to find the "Red Roof Inn," where they had secured a reservation for the next four nights. Everyone was excited. Carol knew that their motel featured a continental breakfast, a pool, and a Jacuzzi. They took the exit, made their way to the parking lot and checked in at the front desk. They were instructed to drive around the side of the motel to their room, an upper unit with a view of a farm.

After they carried up their luggage, Mia and Jon changed and headed to the pool. Carol and Nicole went to the high school to look at the draw. Nicole was due to practice with Erin at 3:30.

When they arrived at the high school, in the corner of the lot stood a familiar motor home.

"Oh, my gosh—the Gunthermans! That's right—the older sister qualified for the sixteens."

Beside the check-in area hung a huge banner: "WELCOME USTA GIRLS FOURTEENS." They checked in and Nicole received a T-shirt and a packet containing the rules. The draw was posed under a canopy. They walked over. Excited, Carol and Nicole started at the top, ran their eyes down, and soon saw the name: 'Nicole Harris –

Milwaukee, Wisconsin.'

Nicole beamed. She was paired to play Pam Mullins from Columbus, Ohio, at 9:00 the following morning. Erin, seeded fourth, was also scheduled to play her opening round at 9:00 against Beth Bayer from Chicago. Of the Wisconsin district, only Erin and Terry were seeded. The seeding for the tournament was as follows:

Singles

1. Sara Luvell - Indianapolis, IN
2. Julie Leftler - Sandusky, OH.
3. Brenda Badad - Chicago, IL
4. Erin Nelson - Glendale, WI
5. Kim Beam - Naperville, IL
6. Ellen Page - Detroit, MI
7. Stacey Hacker - Chicago, IL
8. Bonnie Blake - Battle Creek, MI
9. Hope Collins - Lancing, MI
10. Sadie Pierce - Grand Rapids, MI
11. Deborah Boil - Peoria, IL
12. Linda Blank - Elkhart, IN
13. Diane Sutton - South Bend, IN
14. Sue Martin - Oak Lawn, IL
15. Carol Kaul - Kalamazoo, MI
16. Terry Williams - Brookfield, WI

Nicole found Sara's, Susan's, and Terry's names on the draw. Doubles play included thirty-one teams, with the Smith girls seeded number two.

As it was almost 3:30, Nicole and Carol looked for

Erin. At once a man in his twenties approached. "Hi. I'm Ben Johnson," he began. "My service called Compu-tennis could really help you. What I do is chart your entire match. From this I can provide a four-page analysis of your game—strengths and weaknesses—just where you need to improve. Would you be interested?"

Carol asked him the price. He said $30. Carol asked for his card. She would think about it, she said. As she and Nicole walked off, Carol said, "Wow, I never knew this was so sophisticated."

Erin and her dad appeared. "Hi, Harrises," he said. "The Wisconsin group is over there," he announced, pointing to some tennis courts.

They walked over. The Smiths and the Guntherman girls were on Court One. Ann was not in the tournament, but her older sister Jennifer was playing in the sixteen's. Mrs. Smith, looking very young wearing a bikini top to take advantage of the sun, was picking up balls with a metal hopper. On Court Two were Terry, Susan and Sara. After the greetings, Erin and Nicole took Court Three. Erin decided to forego playing doubles in this tournament, since she was feeling tired again. She recalled how draining it had been playing both singles and doubles last year. Terry and Susan entered to play as a team and on the last minute, Nicole and Sara decided to play as a team as well. Of the group, only the Smiths were seeded.

The girls switched around freely, engaging in different games and drills. At times they matched two players on one side against one person on another, forcing the single person to work harder to compete. Everyone enjoyed the team atmosphere. As the odds were against these girls having to play each other, it made sense to cheer for all Wisconsin players. Each victory would upgrade the district and favorably affect their overall rankings. After about an hour and a half of intense play, the girls had enough. They wished each other good luck and departed.

Back at the motel, Mia and Jon were already changed out of their swimsuits into dry clothes and ready for dinner. As Nicole cleaned up, Carol ordered a pizza. They sat by the pool and enjoyed the pizza and soft drinks, then walked four blocks to an ice-cream shop where each found a favorite flavor. Enjoying their cones, they walked leisurely back to the hotel. Carol, Jon, and Nicole changed into their swimsuits and decided to relax and soak in the Jacuzzi. At 9:00, everyone decided it was time to call it a day; to get a good night's sleep for the long day ahead.

# TAKE THE BALL ON THE RISE

At 7:00 a.m. the phone rang, followed by an alarm clock. Nicole was taking no chances that she might oversleep and not be ready on time. Jon rose quickly too, motivated by the reminder that juice, donuts, cereal, and fresh fruit were available early each morning by the pool, on a first-come-first-served basis.

With Jon gone, the girls got ready, and Nicole did her stretching. Soon Jon came running back. "Hurry up!" he said. "There's a huge assortment! All *kinds* of delicious stuff!"

They laughed and followed Jon back to the pool area. "It's a good thing we have our own Donut Detective!" said Mia. The donuts looked delicious, but Nicole restrained herself and chose a very small one. She decided that the fresh fruit and cereal were better choices that would provide her with more energy. She wasn't very hungry, but knew she needed to fuel her body for the matches ahead.

At 8:15, they drove to the tournament. The facility was packed, and they were happy to spot Erin and her dad. Erin and Nicole warmed up for about twenty-five minutes, and then made their way through the throngs to the main desk. Many of the girls arrived without their parents. Some had come with tennis pros, compliments of well-to-do families. A mom was overheard on the phone, discussing the seeding among other things. "They just don't know the meaning of the word *guest*," she complained. All the "important people—the Luvells, Badads, and Beams—are all here," she said, as she read from a piece of paper. When finished, she filed the paper into her tennis briefcase. Many people openly threw names around. Some outright ignored others. Several parents had computer programs with lists of entrants and information about each. They would enter a name and a complete profile would appear.

Erin told Nicole that the individual profiles are quite thorough. Page one includes a player's vital physical stats. Page two contains the tournament history of the player. Page three is an overview of her strengths and weaknesses. "They even mention things like bad second serve, no backhand, no net game, or even previous ankle injury," explained Erin. One person entered a name and received an error message. "I'm not getting anything on the Henderson girl. She must be a rookie. How can she be out here and not on the computer? Well, she won't be here for long."

"Gosh, this really does seem like a snobbish crowd," said Mia.

Carol shrugged. "Well, we can just set a good example and be kind to everyone," she said.

The director soon called the first-match players, including Nicole who introduced herself to Pam Mullins, a very petite girl from Columbus, Ohio. She was escorted by her mom, who smiled at Nicole and spoke with an accent. Pam, too, had a wooden racquet—the only other player besides Nicole to have one. As they warmed up, Pam missed a few shots and was swift to apologize. She seemed a bit nervous. "No problem," responded Nicole.

After ten minutes they were ready. Nicole started off

hitting the ball well and took a commanding 4-1 lead. Pam hustled on every point, but was no match for Nicole's consistency. At times cheers of the families erupted in the distance as the players competed. With her lead, Nicole attempted to reach the net more than usual. She was rewarded as she scored on several great volleys.

After the first set, Pam told Nicole that she was a first-year fourteen's player. She got into the tournament because the girl a spot above her couldn't come. Although Pam improved in later games, Nicole played well, and won by a score of 6-1, 6-2.

As they reported the score, Pam and her mom shook Nicole's hand and wished her good luck. Nicole did the same, and walked over to her family.

"Boy, they were really nice," said Carol.

"They sure were," said Nicole.

Nicole checked the updated draw. At 1:00, she would next play Candace Barr from Rockford, Illinois. Erin already won 6-1, 6-0 and apparently left the court. None of the other Wisconsin girls were playing yet. Starting to get hungry, Nicole and the family discussed options for lunch. As they walked to the car, the wind started to pick up. Carol chose the local Bob Evans restaurant, with selections closer to a good, home-cooked meal than other fast food options.

"Bob is our man!" Carol declared as they drove off.

They returned by 12:30. Candace, a very tall second-year fourteen, and Nicole were to play on Court One, the stadium court. On the way, Candace said to Nicole, "Please, don't call me Candy."

Nicole nodded.

"I've been called "Candy Barr" way too often!  she added.  Nicole laughed.

"Barr is actually my stepdad's name. He adopted me and that's how I acquired the name.  It was a difficult decision when the judge asked me whether I wanted to change my name."

 "I'm sorry."

"You want to really hear a funny one, Nicole?"

"What's that?"

"My former last name was Kane!"

They both laughed. Candy—or as requested "Candace"— was a delightful girl, a real stitch. Nicole wasn't sure how much to believe, but enjoyed the humorous exchange and went along.

Nicole won the spin and served. She soon realized that Candace, although very easy-going during warm-ups, started to become very serious on the court.  She was a fine player with a solid, all-around game. Every opportunity she was given; she exploited. The match drew even at 3-3. Each girl held serve. However, the major problem wasn't the opponent—it was the wind. On many points, gusts of wind carried balls far from where players hit them. Players found themselves waiting to retrieve balls from adjoining courts. The wind was clearly causing matches to interfere with others.

While Court One presented a retrieval issue only on one

side, Candace and Nicole were each forced to accommodate for the wind. Each soon realized that a ball hit higher and longer allowed the wind to have a greater effect. Sometimes it was even necessary to aim shots out of bounds to get the ball to land in. However, if the wind lapsed temporarily, shots went sailing out of bounds. On several occasions, each girl found herself racing almost onto Court Two to return a ball. Another problem was the serve. Nicole, luckily, did not toss her serves high, which minimized the wind's effect. Candace's service motion, however, required a higher toss and as a consequence was more affected by untimely wind gusts.

Yes, the wind was a problem, but it was a problem for everyone; playing no favorites. Each player had to battle nature's force. Nicole felt fortunate to win the first set 6-4. The second was just as windy, the match just as close. With the score 4-4, Nicole hit two consecutive serves which were caught by the wind and blown from one side of the box to the other—two aces. She continued to play strong, and found herself up, 5-4. Candace was visibly upset. Nature's fury certainly had an adverse effect on her normally consistent game. She rushed through the final game and double-faulted twice, giving Nicole the victory. When they met at the net, Nicole told Candace, "I know that I got some lucky breaks with the wind today!"

"Thanks Nicole. But you earned the match. You played smart with the wind. " she graciously offered.

As they walked to the desk, they heard loud voices

shouting. A roving line judge had overruled a call in the Badad–Simon match on Court Two. The Badad girl had claimed that Simon was foot-faulting. Simon had claimed that Badad was cheating on line calls. With the judge opting to remain on the court for the rest of the match, Badad was on her best behavior, while Simon's confidence was shaken. She double-faulted several times and lost, 6-3,6-3. On the final point, Mr. Simon blurted, "She cheated and intimidated my daughter—it's not fair!"

The girls left the court separately. Mr. Simon greeted his daughter on the walkway, where they met Mr. Badad, a tiny Romanian who wagged a finger in the other's face. "Next time we get you 6-0, 6-0!" he exclaimed, as he turned and stalked off.

The day's results were posted. The "Wisconsin group" had played and represented their district well. Erin, Terry, and Nicole were both 2-0. Susan and Sara were 1-1. Erin would play again tomorrow at 10:00; Nicole at 9:00. They agreed to meet at 8:30 to warm-up. Nicole was scheduled to meet the thirteenth seed, Diane Sutton from South Bend, Indiana.

The Harrises rushed back to the motel, changed into their swimsuits, and took a refreshing swim. Afterwards, they decided to take a trip to the nearby Michigan State University campus. They had heard a lot about the campus. They drove around, and found the tennis courts, the stadium, the library, and the student union. They spotted a McAlister's Deli and gave it a try. The kids had never been on a college campus and Mia had only been on the University of Wisconsin–Milwaukee's campus once, for Carol's graduation, when she received her nursing degree.

"I want to go to college, because they have so many sports facilities and food places," Jon said full of excitement.

Nicole laughed. "In college you have to study, too, you know."

"I will," said Jon.

Their waitress, a nursing student, told the group that she loved going to school at MSU. Jon told her that Carol is a nurse. The young woman shared that she intended to work in the nursery, with babies, just like Carol. "Your name isn't Carol, is it?" asked Jon. Everyone laughed.

Back at the motel, the Harrises ended the day, sitting by the pool, telling stories. Mia always had wonderful, interesting memories to share from her past.

They were all up by 7:00 a.m. Jon rushed to make his 'donut run' while everyone got ready. Sitting poolside, Nicole noticed that there was only a slight breeze, quite a contrast from the gusts of wind yesterday. Nicole breathed a sigh of relief. They enjoyed fruit, cereal, muffins, and juice. Jon however, focused on his newly proclaimed breakfast 'donut diet'.

At 8:30, Nicole met Erin. Most of the courts were already taken, but they luckily found one at the far end. As they warmed up, Erin looked sluggish, but improved quickly. At 8:50 they ended their warm-up and wished each other good luck.

Nicole made her way to the desk. Diane, her opponent, was wearing a very stylish green Notre Dame sweat suit with the little leprechaun logo on the front. They walked to the court.

"I really like your outfit, Diane."

"Thanks. I live quite close to Notre Dame. I've wanted to go to school there since I was a little girl. When I was four years old, my Dad took me to my first football game on the campus. I fell in love with the school and all the tradition. It's really cool!"

The girls warmed up. After only a few minutes, Diane asked Nicole if she was ready, and they started their match. Nicole won the spin and served first. As Nicole made her first toss, she couldn't help but notice how much calmer it was today, than yesterday. Her first serve was long, but the second was on the mark. Diane made a powerful return, forcing Nicole to her left across the baseline to play the ball. With no time to set herself, she planted her left foot, coiled, and made contact, falling through the ball. Her return, toward the middle of the court, was met in mid-air by a charging Diane, who directed a volley deep to the opposite corner, for a winner.

Once again, Nicole's second serve proved to be her downfall. Without getting a racquet on a return, Nicole found herself down 0-15. As Nicole readied to serve, she knew she must get her first serve in, or she would be in for a tough time. With Diane far back, Nicole focused extra effort to make sure the ball was in. Diane approached, and the two got into a baseline-to-baseline rally. After twelve blistering hits, Nicole's shot went wide left.

On her next serve, Nicole caught the ball squarely and sent it just inside the service box. A lunging Diane barely got a racquet on the ball, and her shot sailed into the net; 15-30. Nicole then opted to use her second serve as a first offering. Diane sensed this tactical change and moved up amid Nicole's service motion. This placed her in a great position to pound the ball deep for a winner; 15-40. A frustrated Nicole hit her next serve long. Now Nicole was forced to hit her weaker serve, with Diane already moving up. The serve struck the middle of the service box, and Diane was all over it. She once again crushed the weak ball with another winner, deep to Nicole's left. Diane took game one.

Diane's service game was far superior to Nicole's. If she didn't get her first ball in, her second serve proved to be a huge weapon with ample spin. It struck the court and exploded, kicking high and deep. While Nicole was normally adept at returning serve, the blend of the serves put enormous pressure on her. Meanwhile, Nicole's second serve continued to provide Diane with opportunities to exploit. As for baseline play, Nicole held her own. Her consistency exceeded that of her opponent. During long rallies Nicole sparkled and won more than her share of points, but Diane took the first set, 6-2.

Down 3-0 in the second set, Nicole fought tooth and nail to tie the score at 3-3. However, her service continued to falter and Diane attacked and took advantage of the weakness, winning the last three games to take the match.

As they approached the net, a dejected Nicole could identify the problem, but felt helpless, unsure how to correct it. Her serve was her serve; it's all she knew. Nicole's service game clearly led to her first tournament loss. Not only was her second serve weak, but Nicole also needed to improve her first-serve percentage. Diane was a fine player—the thirteenth seed—but, excluding the service issue, Nicole knew she wasn't far behind. She realized it was important to focus on the next match and not dwell on this recent loss. She was still in the running, but no longer in the main draw. Many fine players have successfully made their way from the back draw to still achieve a fifth place tournament finish. This was now Nicole's new goal.

Nicole reported the score and saw her family. Carol praised her ground strokes.

"Nicole, you're going to be fine," said Mia. "You just have a few hurdles to get over. Remember—Rome wasn't built in a day."

Nicole smiled. "Thanks," she said.

At 2:00, Nicole would next play Julie Polk from Downers Grove, Illinois. The Harrises returned to the motel for Nicole to clean up and change, and then went to eat at the local Burger King. Nicole was still thinking about the match as they waited for their food. Mia and Carol tried to distract her, at least for the moment, but Nicole was deep in thought.

They leisurely enjoyed lunch. The cool air felt nice. After, they rested back at the motel, while Jon jumped into the pool. By 1:45 they returned to the tournament and Nicole did some stretching. At 2:10 a court opened up and the call sounded for Nicole and Julie, a first-year fourteen and a very short but stocky girl. As they rallied, Julie used her legs extremely well and stepped into every shot.

Julie won the right to serve. Nicole took a deep breath and offered a silent prayer. "God, please help me to be confident in my abilities and play my best," she said.

Julie served. Nicole readied herself, ran up, shuffled her feet, stepped fully into the ball, and made a terrific return that left Julie reeling. Julie's next serve was answered almost the same, with Nicole's shot bouncing at Julie's feet and handcuffing her return.

The next two points were lengthy ones as both girls hit an array of baseline shots. Julie mixed her first and second serves to keep Nicole off balance, prompted by Nicole's two great returns to start the match. Julie served,15-40. Nicole lined up her feet and smashed the ball down the line. Julie ran over and lobbed. Nicole back-pedaled two steps, set herself, and hit an overhead winner. Game one was in the books.

Nicole was relaxed. Once again, her confidence returned. She played her normal game, hit her first serve every time, went for broke, and let the results be what they may. Nicole's first five serves were on the mark. She won three of the points. At 40-30 she missed her first serve. Julie returned her second sharply down the line. As Nicole sprinted to her right, Julie approached, and a running Nicole hit the ball short and across the court. The ball cleared the net just under

Julie's reach, giving Nicole the game and a 2-0 lead.

The pace and accuracy of Nicole's serve in this match, made her tough to break. Her service return continued to dominate, denying Julie a service advantage. These two factors helped Nicole, who only hours earlier had felt dejected. Julie continued to be very consistent from the baseline, but when Nicole's shots forced Julie to take some pace off the ball, it left Nicole with some easy approach shots and a road to the net. Nicole kept the pressure on. After taking the first set 6-3, she won the last four games of the second set for a 6-2 score. Nicole had played her best match thus far and she knew it.

Nicole congratulated Julie, and then made their way to the desk. This was Julie's second loss. She was eliminated. Nicole would play Melody Hart from Detroit, Michigan at 9:30. Erin won her two matches, was now 4-0 and in the final eight. Terry lost and, like Nicole, was 3-1. She and Nicole still had a chance to play for fifth, coming from the back draw. Susan and Sara had been ousted, each finishing 2-2. Wisconsin had fared well. Nicole congratulated the other Wisconsin girls on their efforts. "Erin, great job!" offered her dad, hugging her. "We're going to make it. I mean—you're going to make it!" He was referring to a slot in the nationals, since Erin was in the final eight. He felt confident that this win guaranteed her a spot in the nationals. Susan and Sara would have a few days to rest until the doubles started.

Erin's dad congratulated Nicole. "You really came back strong after your earlier match! Way to be tough!!"

"Thanks Mr. Nelson." Nicole's family was excited. Jon, Carol, and Gram smiled and gave her big hugs. "The construction in Italy has definitely started," said Gram. Nicole smiled.

It was time to go back, take a well-deserved jump in the pool, and relax for the rest of the day. Erin's dad agreed to let her join the Harrises for some fun. The girls and Jon had a great time. Jon won the "who could swim the farthest underwater" contest. For Nicole, the day had been stressful, providing both highs and lows. Today, she learned the importance of finding an answer for a loss, and gained a better understanding of her abilities as she played with more determination. Yes, Rome definitely *was* under major construction. After a fine dinner at Luigi's, a local Italian restaurant, the Harrises took Erin back to her hotel and decided to retire early. The local news predicted more heat and sun. Nicole realized that playing solid tennis involved more than just outplaying an opponent. It also involved surviving the elements.

# POINT YOUR FRONT FOOT

At 7:15, the wakeup call came. Carol jumped up, and turned off Nicole's clock. Today many of the players would learn their fate. With the exception of the top four spots, the back draw would feed into the main draw. A win for Erin would place her in the semifinals—and for the most part, she probably already had earned a spot on the list for the nationals. More wins could find her seeded. Yes, much was on the line today.

Jon made his morning donut run, and they sat around the pool for breakfast. Carol suggested that Nicole stay away from the donuts, if just for today. This was not easy, since Jon had chosen a chocolate-covered bismark, Nicole's favorite.

By 8:40 they were at the tournament. Erin was nowhere to be found, but Nicole bumped into Terry, who told her that Erin had a headache. Terry and Nicole warmed up for the 9:30 matches. About 9:10 Erin arrived. She and her dad warmed up quickly. Erin looked weary, and didn't say very much.

At 9:30 the girls were called, and wished each other luck. Nicole introduced herself to Melody Hart from Detroit, who stood about six feet tall—some four inches taller than Nicole—and had a very dark complexion and long, dark hair. As they headed to Court Three, Melody wasn't very chatty. Nicole figured that, with so much on the line, she was focusing on the match. She didn't blame her.

After a brief warm-up, Melody won the chance to serve. Nicole sighed deeply, and readied herself. The offering was perfect, and Nicole hit it squarely into the net. Nicole hit the next serve wide. Disappointed with her start, she repeated to herself the words "in, in, in." She returned the next serve. The ball hit the net and fell limply on Melody's side—an improvement, but not the crisp return Nicole hoped for. With the next serve long, Melody resorted to her second serve for the first time. The serve came, spinning but certainly not with the exploding kick of Diane Sutton's. Nicole hit the ball on the rise, driving it down the line. As Melody ran over, Nicole approached the net and anticipating the cross-court shot, and hit a crisp volley to the opposite corner. The first game was tied up 30-30.

As she lined up to serve, Melody seemed upset. She walked away for a moment, then came back. Nicole smacked the next serve at Melody's feet. She leaped, but to no avail. The ball hit her foot and trickled away. She was down 30-40. Nicole had won the last three points.

Melody took a deep sigh, and served—a fault. Nicole reacted to her second serve with an under-spin return, short and down the line. Melody raced over, but hit a weak return down the line. Nicole  followed  her own shot in,  and intercepted Melody's  return  with a backhand volley to the opposite court for a winner.

As they switched sides, Melody began  to talk to herself. Nicole hoped her own first serve would be sharp enough to complement her return game. Her first attempt was perfect— an ace just inside the box. Nicole now felt confident. She knew she *would* play her best both serving or returning serve. However, Melody although dejected, was determined to fight back. The match grew very competitive, with each player hitting high-level shots. When Melody left Nicole for dead on a lob and ran in for the weak return, Nicole didn't give up on the point. She ran around the ball sending her own topspin lob just over the outstretched racquet of Melody. On the next volley, Melody came to the net only to meet a rocket from Nicole at the baseline. Melody lifted her racquet in front of her face. The ball ricocheted off, across the net, for a winner.

The many short balls and chances to approach made for skirmishes at the net, with the players volleying several times before one took the point. Nicole won the first set 6-4. Melody took the second 6-4. The third set was tight as well. With a double-fault by Melody, Nicole took a 6-5 lead and would serve for the match. The girls had been playing for more than two-and-a-half hours. Nicole took a deep breath, tossed the ball, and hit a rocket that handcuffed Melody, leaving no return. The next serve hit the line just inside the box for an ace; 30-0.

As Nicole readied herself, Melody retreated and moved around to prepare herself and perhaps distract Nicole. Nicole opted for her second serve. The ball barely cleared the net, leaving Melody an unexpected short offering since she had been standing deep behind the baseline. She raced up, returning the ball high and short. Nicole ran in, and set herself. As the ball landed and rose waist high into her power zone, she blasted it smoothly and flatly into the opposite court.

Nicole had triple match point. Winning one of the next three points would earn her the victory and entry into the next round. Nicole adjusted her headband, and readied herself. Her serve was returned sharply across court. Nicole quickly moved over, set her feet, stepped, and hit the ball down the line—perfect, two feet short of the baseline. Melody ran over, prepared her backhand, and drove the ball powerfully. The ball grazed the top of the net and sailed beyond the baseline.

Nicole was calm as she approached the net, shook Melody's hand, and congratulated her for a fine match. The match could have gone either way. Melody was out of the tournament. Nicole was still alive for another match. Erin also came from behind to win, 7-5, 6-3. Now, 5-0, she was in the semifinals. Terry also advanced. Like Nicole, she was 4-1 and still alive from the back draw. Nicole would next face Bonnie Blake, the eighth seed from Battle Creek, Michigan at 2:30.

With two hours before the match, the Harris family went out for a quick bite to eat, and then returned to the motel, where Nicole showered and changed into dry clothes. Carol applied cool compresses to Nicole's forehead and wrists to accelerate her cool-down. Nicole had already played for more than two-and-a-half hours, and was slated to play again after a very short recuperation time. As she nibbled her sandwich, Nicole looked tired to Carol, who voiced her concern. Nicole however, insisted she was fine and would be ready to play.

Back at the tournament after receiving her court assignment, Nicole warmed up with Bonnie, the eighth seed who lost to the top seed, Sara Luvell from Indianapolis, 6-1, 6-2. Both girls seemed tired and sluggish. When they were ready, Nicole served first—a finely placed effort that Bonnie returned into the net. After Nicole followed with an unusual double fault, Bonnie smartly returned a serve and both players hit shots from the baseline before Nicole hit a forehand wide. Bonnie hit a winner off Nicole's second serve making the score 15-40, but hit Nicole's next serve long. Then Bonnie hit a weak shot, but Nicole did not take advantage of the easy approach and hit the shot wide, giving Bonnie the first game.

Nicole won game two, in spite of two unforced errors, but Bonnie had three. With her solid overall game, Bonnie probably had a competitive edge in almost every aspect of the game. A second-year fourteen, she had been on the circuit for more than five years. Today, despite her experience, she was scarcely playing up to her ability.

The match continued, amid many unforced errors. Both players seemed to mimic each other and took turns making mistakes. Nicole hit balls on the run that she would normally have time to set up for. On one occasion, she hit an easy forehand cross court, unaware that Bonnie was racing up for an easy volley. Bonnie hit a waist-high offering with under-spin that left the ball squarely in the net. Both girls looked tired, and made errors they normally would not. Three demanding days of tennis seemed to take their toll. Nicole now realized that to win the Westerns, it not only took talent, but great endurance and concentration.

Bonnie won the first set 6-3. At 5-2 in the second, with Nicole serving, the game went to deuce. The next point, the longest rally of the match, ended with Nicole hitting a backhand into the net. At match point, Nicole hit an approach shot down the line and followed it to the net. Bonnie countered with a perfect backhand down the line. Nicole reached out, but the ample topspin made the ball drop below Nicole's outstretched racquet for a winner.

The error-plagued match was over. Bonnie would advance. The two girls shook hands at the net and returned to the tournament desk. It was now nearly four o'clock. Most of the scores were in. Checking the draw, Nicole and her family were disappointed to learn that Erin lost to top seed Sara Luvell, 6-4, 7-5. Erin would play tomorrow for third place against Julie Leftler, while Sara would meet Brenda Badad for the championship. Terry also lost, and like Nicole, finished the tournament 4-2.

With the singles matches completed, a computer would analyze the information and render rankings. All matches within the section for the entire year, since January, would be factored in. The top sixteen in the section would advance to play in the national tournament.

Later in the day, the doubles would start, with Nicole and Sara Cummings playing together. It was readily apparent to Carol and Mia that Nicole was very sad. As long as you can swing a racquet you can determine your fate, thought Nicole, but now it was completely out of her control and up to the computer. Although her last match, ended with a loss, Mia advised Nicole to take into consideration the entire schedule she had played since she started in May.

"You have improved tremendously in three short months. Be proud of what you have accomplished," she emphasized.

Carol echoed the sentiment.

With Nicole slated to start doubles at 5:15, the Harrises found a shady spot to rest. Precisely at 5:00, Sara and Nicole received their call. They would play the sixth seeds, Carol Kaul and Pam Clinton, from Kalamazoo, Michigan. They were two talented girls who had played together for several years and worked beautifully together as a team. The Michigan girls took a quick command of the match. Although Sara and Nicole had some fine points, they were not enough. They ended up losing 6-2, 6-2.

By this time, Nicole was extremely tired. She now understood why Erin opted out of the doubles. Nicole and Sara would again play at 9:00 tomorrow morning, against an opponent yet to be determined. It was already 6:30. Their hotel was hosting a picnic and barbeque until 7:00. They rushed back and found the pool area crowded. The food looked great—an assortment of hamburgers, hotdogs, potato salad, chips, Jell-O, pickles, and popsicles. They filled their plates, sat by the pool, and relaxed. Once again Jon created a hotdog "masterpiece."

It was nice to end the day with a delicious picnic,

compliments of the Red Roof. If Nicole and Sara lost tomorrow, it would be Nicole's last day in the tournament. They decided to wait until after the match to determine if they needed to pack quickly in order to leave in time for checkout. It had been a long day. They all retired early.

Again the wake-up call came at 7:30 a.m. Jon, already up and dressed, readied himself for what might be his last donut run.

"I'll meet all of you at the pool," he called as he left in a rush.

Carol and Mia washed up. Nicole dressed and then stretched. Within ten minutes, the three were out the door, and enjoyed their breakfast as the sun came up over the roof. Carol went back to the room to get things together, in case a quick exit was needed. They left for the tournament and arrived at 8:30.

Erin, her father, Terry, Susan, Sara, along with the entire Smith family, gathered on Courts Four and Five. Erin confided to Nicole that she didn't feel well, and was glad this would be her last match. The doubles players were called. Sara and Nicole would play Claire Johnson and Midge Sanders, from Detroit, who lost to the fourth seed by a 6-3, 6-4 margin yesterday. Since each team had lost its first match, a loss today would mean elimination from the tournament.

The girls took the court and warmed up. Claire served first. The first game was very close, and very long. Several times all four girls found themselves face to face at the net and produced close-up sequences of four to six volleys before each point ended. After winning the first game, the Detroit team took control of game two, their superior strategy and teamwork readily apparent. Seeming to find a soft spot between Nicole and Sara, they turned their lead into a victory of 6-1.

The second set became more competitive, as Sara and Nicole better coordinated their efforts. However, after winning a series of eight straight points, the Detroit team secured the second set 6-4. Sara and Nicole congratulated their opponents and made their way to the desk. Nicole thanked Sara for playing with her and voiced her disappointment. Nicole and her family hurried back to the motel, where Nicole showered and changed. The Harrises packed their suitcases and loaded them into the car.

The championship and third-place singles would begin soon, and Nicole wanted to lend Erin some support, so the Harrises headed back. On Court One, Sara Luvell would play Brenda Badad. On Court Two, Erin would play Julie Leftler. A big crowd was on hand for both matches.

Erin served first, and started out with a double fault. She fought back, but Julie broke her serve and won the game. During game two, Erin didn't seem to hustle after balls she normally would have. "Come on Erin—let's go!" her dad yelled. Soon she was down 3-0.

On the bench drinking water, getting ready to change sides, Erin motioned to her dad. He ran down to the court and sat with her. Afterwards, they both got up and walked over to Julie. Erin was not feeling well and was too sick to continue. She would have to forfeit. Erin shook her hand and they left the court together. Nicole ran up and put her arm around Erin, who was trying to hold back the tears. Nicole and Carol found a shady spot to sit Erin down, as her father talked to the officials. Carol applied some cool compresses that seemed to help. After a few minutes Erin rallied, as her dad returned. He and Carol talked for a few minutes about Erin. The Nelsons decided to go back to their motel for Erin to shower and rest. The Harrises said goodbye. Nicole gave Erin a big hug. Mr. Nelson thanked Nicole and Carol and wished them a safe trip home. As they left, the tournament director posted the final standings for the sectional singles. Except for numbers one and two that were presently playing, he told them, the list was set in stone:

<u>Singles</u>

1. Sara Luvell - Indianapolis, IN
2. Brenda Badad - Chicago, IL
3. Julie Leftler - Sandusky, OH
4. Erin Nelson - Glendale, WI
5. Stacey Hacker - Chicago, IL
6. Hope Collins - Lancing, MI
7. Kim Beam - Naperville, IL
8. Linda Blank - Elkhart, IN
9. Diane Sutton - South Bend, IN
10. Ellen Page - Detroit, MI
11. Sadie Pierce – Grand Rapids, MI
12. Sue Martin - Oak Lawn, IL
13. Deborah Boil - Peoria, IL

14. Bonnie Blake - Battle Creek, MI
15. Terry Williams - Brookfield, WI
16. Mary Stills - Chicago, IL
17. Nicole Harris - Milwaukee, WI
18. Melody Hart - Detroit, MI
19. Ann Hubert - Gurney, IL
20. Sally Horton - Evansville, IN

Nicole was very surprised. She finished seventeenth! Erin was fourth; Terry fifteenth. As two of the top 16, Erin and Terry both secured a spot in the national tournament to be played in San Diego. Nicole looked to congratulate Terry, but she and Susan were nowhere to be found. Nicole saw the Smith girls, who had advanced to the doubles round of eight, and wished them luck. Carol, Mia, and Jon told Nicole how proud they were of her and of how well she had played.

"For you to be seventeenth out of 128 girls is amazing. Truly, amazing!" Mia said as they walked to the car. It had been an incredible four days—an experience the Harrises would never forget.

It was a unanimous decision; everyone wanted to get home as quick as possible. To accomplish this, the goal was try to make it home with only two stops for gas, the first accompanied by lunch, and the second, dinner. They made it to Battle Creek, before stopping for gas and to eat. Delegated the one to choose, Jon picked Dairy Queen. With the fast service, they were fed and back on the road in no time and made their last stop just outside Chicago. Mia said she couldn't wait to get home and have a home-cooked meal tomorrow. It sure was fun eating out, but there's nothing like home-cooked meals to nourish the body and warm the heart.

By 8:30, just as it was getting dark, they pulled in the driveway. It was comforting to drive safely into the garage. They were home, sweet home, at last. After they unloaded the car, Nicole, Jon, and Mia slipped into their "jammies." It was great to be settled back into their home and everyone was looking forward to sleeping in their own beds. Since tomorrow was Saturday, Carol would be able to get some rest. She didn't have to work until Sunday night.

Carol slept well after the long trip. At 7:00 however, she was up and wasted no time starting the first of several loads of wash. Nicole slept a bit later than usual, and was up by 9 am. She couldn't wait to call Mr. Novak with the tournament news, but first she wanted to check on Erin. Erin reassured Nicole that she was feeling much better. After a restful weekend, she planned to start practicing for the nationals. The two girls made plans to see a movie on Tuesday. They planned to talk more then. As for Mr. Novak, he was excited to hear Nicole's news. He told her he was so proud of her.

"Nicole, next year you have a great chance to get to San Diego. Just keep the faith," he advised.

# IT'S CONTROL VERSUS POWER

J on's best friend Jimmy really missed him. He rang the doorbell bright and early to see if Jon could play. Jimmy and Jon built a fort in the backyard. Cindy rode her bike over to Nicole's house. Then, she and Nicole decided to go for a long bike ride. For Nicole, it felt good to play and hang-out with her friend Cindy, after the past week's pressure. Throughout the day, Nicole's thoughts wandered, thinking about all the girls from the various sections across the country, getting ready for the nationals. Nicole was sad and she had to admit, quite envious, but realized there was more to life than tennis. She reminded herself that she was so fortunate that she had so many other activities to occupy her time and keep her busy for the rest of the summer.

Later that night the family went to church, arriving early, because Nicole wanted to light another candle for her dad. In addition, she intended to light another candle in thanksgiving; to express her gratitude for her wonderful tennis success she experienced this year and for the memorable family trip to Michigan. After church, they stopped to greet and chat with many of the other families, just like every week. Dr. and Mrs. Stanwood and Jenny were excited to hear about Nicole's tournament. An especially impressed Dr. Stanwood gave Nicole a big hug, then told Carol that everyone had missed her at the hospital. He quickly reminded Jon that there were only three short weeks before the lake vacation. Once back home, Mia put the finishing touches on the home-cooked meal she and the others craved. Everyone sat down to enjoy Mia's famous beef roast, gravy, browned potatoes, and buttered corn. She surprised everyone with a family favorite dessert—strawberry short cake. Every bite was thoroughly enjoyed by all.

On Sunday, Nicole and Jon worked together in the yard, cutting the grass, trimming the bushes, picking weeds from the flowerbeds, and watering the plants. The two were very proud of their efforts, as they noticed how tidy and well manicured their property looked. Normally, Carol took care of the outside, but Nicole knew that their mom needed a break after all she had done. Jon and Nicole felt very productive and decided they would assume this responsibility from now on. It would give Mom a break and besides, they enjoyed working outside together.

School was only a month away. Before long, Nicole would start eighth grade, her final year at St. Elizabeth's. Her teacher this year would be the famed Sister Clara, a very kind, deeply religious woman whom all the kids adored. Nicole could hardly wait. She knew her last year at St. Elizabeth would be a lot of fun.

On Monday morning, Carol arrived home just as Nicole and Jonathan were getting up.

When Carol was sleeping, the kids always tried to be quiet or play outside the house. They had a fun week planned. Today, Nicole and Carrie decided to pack a picnic lunch and spend the day at the park. Tuesday, Nicole planned to go see a movie with Erin. Thursday night, she intended to sleep at Cindy's house with four girls from school. On Friday, Nicole would spend the day baby-sitting for Jenny Stanwood.

Late in the day, after dinner, the phone rang. It was Mr. Nelson's brother, asking for Carol.

"Erin's been taken to the hospital. She was practicing with her pro, when she became very sick, and fainted. We took her to the emergency room and the doctors decided to admit her for some tests. Erin asked me to let Nicole know she won't be able to see a movie tomorrow. Test results are pending."

"Please give Erin and the Nelsons our best and tell them that we will be praying for Erin," Carol said. "We'll come to see Erin tomorrow at the hospital."

Carol gave the family the news. A very sad Nicole hoped Erin would recover quickly.

Two hours later, Mr. Nelson's brother called again. In a barely audible voice he told Carol, "I just want to let you know that Erin passed away about an hour ago. The doctors said she had an aneurism. They just couldn't save her. We'll be in touch."

With that, he hung up. A shocked Carol hung onto the phone, as the others gathered around.

"Mom—what's happened?" asked Nicole.

Carol hung up. She put her arm around Nicole, and started to cry. "Honey, Erin just passed away at the hospital about an hour ago. I'm really sorry."

After a period of shock, they all cried together. They made their way to the living room and sat together, hugging one another for comfort. Carol asked everyone to join hands and led the family in a prayer. She thanked God for the gift of Erin's life and expressed gratitude for the time they had with her.

"God works in mysterious ways and sometimes it is difficult to understand why sad things happen, especially to good people like Erin and her family," she said.

Nicole sobbed softly, nodding her head. It was a difficult lesson to learn at any age.

That night, Carol took Nicole a glass of milk along with some homemade peanut butter cookies as a special treat. She decided to retire early for the night. It had been a very emotional day. Nicole told her mother it felt like her heart was breaking.

"Erin was so special, Mom. We really got along so well. I'm really going to miss her!" Nicole told her Mom as she wiped away her tears.

Erin's wake was three days later at the local funeral home. Hundreds of people attended. Many of the junior tennis players came to pay their respect, along with their parents. Floral bouquets filled the room with sweet, heady fragrances. To view Erin was difficult for Nicole. Her parents decorated the casket with many of her tennis memorabilia. Erin's trophy from the Wisconsin Closed and the fourth-place Western Closed stood on a nearby table. The Nelsons were glad to see Nicole, and Erin's mother cried as soon as she saw her. They thanked the Harrises for their support and beautiful flower arrangement.

On Friday, after a beautiful service, Erin was laid to rest. It was a rainy day, but it did not stop more than two hundred people from attending. Afterwards, the family hosted a reception and buffet luncheon at Pandl's, in Fox Point. After everyone finished eating, attendees were invited to come up to the microphone to share something special about Erin and how she had touched their lives. After a few minutes, Nicole walked up.

"I only got to know Erin about three months ago," she said. "Since that time we became great friends. We shared super times together. Erin was a terrific tennis player—not only a great player but a kind person, a true friend. I was somewhat new to tennis this year, and she took me under her wing and helped me. This was truly remarkable for a junior tennis player, since we all compete against each other. She encouraged me and readily complimented my play. I respected her more than anyone I know. When I play tennis, I hope I can emulate her caring attitude and the way she treated others. I know she's in heaven and smiling down on us all right now!"

With that, Nicole brushed a visible tear from her eye and sat down.

Saturday's newspaper featured an article celebrating Erin's life. The Harrises made a donation for the Mass on Saturday at St. Elizabeth's in Erin's honor. Nicole lit a special candle for Erin, right next to her dad's.

On Wednesday, five days later, at 7:00, the Harrises' doorbell rang. Carol was surprised to see Mr. Nelson.

"Hi Carol. Can I come in?"

"Of course. Come in. Sit down."

"Mr. Nelson, what a surprise! It's good to see you," Mia remarked from a chair nearby, where she was knitting, then quietly left the room for the kitchen, to let them speak privately.

"How are you and the family holding up?" Carol asked.

"It's tough." He took a deep breath, and continued. "First, I want to thank you for the flowers and all your assistance. Nicole was incredible at the funeral."

Mia entered with a glass of lemonade for Mr. Nelson. He nodded, took a long sip, then went on. "I would like to tell you the main reason for my visit. I am on the Western sectional committee, but I don't want to mix politics and feelings. Nonetheless, there is currently one spot available on the sectional roster, a spot open for a deserving young lady in the girls 14's. Nicole was technically the first alternate. We would very much like to endorse your daughter for the spot. Personally, I feel she deserves it. I've watched her. Her approach to the game and her demeanor are impressive. She's an athlete, but at the same time she's a lady."

Nicole, who had overhead the conversation, stepped into the living room.

"Can I please go, Mom?? Pleeeeeaase?

"It would be nice, but it just isn't in the budget," Carol sadly told Nicole, and then added, "California sure is a long way from here!"

Nicole agreed, but then Mr. Nelson broke in. "That part has already been considered. I want to pay for the trip. I have already taken the liberty of making reservations for Nicole and her favorite rooting section—her family." He pulled out some tickets. "These are for the flights, hotel, and even tickets for the San Diego Zoo. I couldn't get SeaWorld, but I intend to try again tomorrow. Would you please accept?"

There was a long, heavy silence.

"It's something my wife and I want to do in Erin's memory. All she did was talk about Nicole. Sometimes we think Nicole was the only true friend she ever had. For Erin to have been blessed with Nicole's friendship—well, it means a lot to us. It would really mean a lot to my wife and me if you would accept our offer, please? For my wife and me?"

Mia asked Carol to join her in the kitchen. Mia took a deep breath, and let out a long sigh.

"All our lives we have never taken a dime from anyone. We worked for everything we have. Don't look a gift horse in the mouth. Sometimes you get lucky in life. Besides, it is not merely luck. Nicole was a good friend and now she can do something just as wonderful in Erin's memory. When I was twelve I loved tennis. I was the county champ, just like Nicole. But I was never able to advance because of time and money. I knew my family needed me. Since that time, I have often wondered, and dreamed the 'what if' dream. Nicole has those dreams. I've seen it in her eyes. Besides, life is fickle; Nicole may never get another chance to get this close to her dream. Let's live the dream. Let's give it our best."

They walked back into the living room and accepted Mr. Nelson's offer. Carol's mind was already racing as she blurted out, "I think I can trade vacation weeks with Susan at work. But we'll have to give up our week at the lake that we had planned."

"Are you kidding? Can we really go? I can't believe it!" exclaimed Nicole.

Mr. Nelson looked directly at Nicole. He couldn't help smiling.

"Here is an itinerary for the trip. Oh, by the way Nicole—here is a special one for you. I know that you make the most of everything, including your basic tennis equipment, but this is the nationals we are talking about. So, I took the liberty of setting up some lessons and I think you can use some new racquets and equipment to give you a bit more of a competitive advantage. Don't worry, Mrs. Nelson and I intend to pay for all of this, as well."

With a warm smile, he handed Nicole a packet. "Here is your training schedule at the tennis club. You only have twenty-six days until San Diego."

With that, Mr. Nelson announced that he must go. He asked Nicole if she would walk him out to his car. Outside, many of the neighborhood kids were standing around admiring the car—a new Mercedes, so odd in this vicinity. He greeted the group of children and popped open the trunk.

"I have a few things for you, Nicole."

He handed a dumbfounded Nicole several new tennis outfits, headbands, four graphite racquets monogrammed E.N., and a new, spacious tennis bag. "This stuff should help. I'll stay in touch," he winked. "Good luck, young lady!"

Close to tears, he ducked into the car and drove off. As

Nicole watched him drive off, the kids crowded around her.

"Who was that?" one boy asked.

Nicole looked at him. "A friend," she quietly said.

Nicole was quite embarrassed as she brought in all the equipment. Her family simply could not believe such generosity. Nicole surveyed her schedule. "Oh, my goodness! I have no time to waste. My first lesson at the club is tomorrow at 11:00 a.m."

Mia smiled. "No problem. I've got transportation covered. Mia's Taxi, at your service, Miss!"

They all smiled.

The next morning, Nicole woke up very excited, her thoughts racing about her opportunity to work with a pro and practice tennis, the game she loved. Going to the nationals as a first-year fourteen felt like a dream. She felt honored. But it was an honor she would gladly forsake; if it would bring back her dear friend, Erin.

Mia dropped her off at the club about ten minutes early. Nicole gave her a quick kiss on the cheek, jumped out, and waved good-bye. "I'll be back in about three hours," Mia shouted through the open window.

Toting a water jug, a can of balls, and two racquets— Erin's and her own—Nicole approached the plush country club. At the door, a female security guard stopped her, and asked her name. Mrs. Nelson appeared from around the corner, at the perfect time.

"This is Nicole Harris," she said, "She will be here for the next month. Please add her name to our guest list. Please give her full access to the facility anytime she wants, whether we are here or not."

She greeted Nicole with a big hug. Their eyes met. Both fought back tears. "Nicole, the courts are this way," she added. "Follow me."

There she introduced Nicole to Jeff Sanders, Erin's pro who had agreed to work with Nicole to prepare her for the nationals.

He shook her hand warmly. "Hi, Nicole. Do you remember me from Erin's house?"

"I sure do, Jeff."

He showed Nicole around the club, and told her about the special program he had designed for her. It would include a test and some psychological, mental toughness training, Nautilus weight training, an exercise routine, diet counseling, drill work, matches with boys in the 16's, and finally a player asset/strengths strategy.

"The Nelson family and I wanted to provide you with some comprehensive information that will afford you the best chance to succeed in San Diego." He continued. "The program will be twenty-four sessions, six a week. Today I will get you started with each component of the program and introduce you to some of the others who will work with you. On the court, I will work with you. I will evaluate every match you play here, and may stop a game to reinforce a lesson or strategy. Are you ready to get started?"

"I sure am. And Jeff, thanks for doing this for me!"

After meeting four others who would assist Jeff with the

outlined program, Nicole was given two books describing tennis fundamentals and theory. Nicole glanced at the titles and smiled. When asked why, she replied, "I love tennis books. I read both of these books about six months ago."

The four exchanged glances and grinned.

"It appears you're already a step ahead," said Jeff. "Let's see how much of the game you understand. I want you to take a short 'tennis test' I give to all my new students."

Nicole spent the next thirty minutes poring over fifty questions on rules, strategy, and stroke selection—basically, a tennis IQ test.

"How did I do?" she asked as he reviewed her answers.

Nicole scored 95%—only one wrong answer.

"Wow, Nicole! You *are* one smart young lady!"

With strength training an essential part of tennis, Nicole visited the fitness center. Here Mike Lewis, a personal-fitness instructor, adjusted Nicole's settings on about a dozen Nautilus machines. To prevent injury, she would start out slowly, using relatively low weights with multiple repetitions. In due time, the weight would be increased.

The regimen was intended to work all of Nicole's muscle groups, designed specifically with tennis in mind. When she finished, they returned to the main entrance, where Nicole met four boys. As she was introduced, Nicole couldn't help but notice Phillip, the boy Erin had a crush on, whom Nicole had seen at the funeral.

Jeff explained, "These boys are in the sixteen's and will play matches with you! They'll give you some great competition. They all hit the ball really hard and will run you all over the court! Most importantly, the fast paced matches will teach you to think and respond quickly! I expect you to rise to the occasion and elevate your level of play!"

The next stop was to meet Sally Roth, the club's nurse on staff to assist with first aid if needed. Also a nutritional counselor, Sally would evaluate Nicole's diet and recommend changes for peak performance. She gave Nicole a quick lesson about nutrition and healthy eating. She showed Nicole a picture of the Food Pyramid which depicted the various food groups along with the recommended daily servings. She encouraged natural foods, especially fresh fruits and vegetables as well as lean meats for protein, along with complex carbohydrates. She told Nicole that these are the keys to healthy eating and maximizing energy for optimal performance.

The nutrition lesson over, Sally reviewed the importance of stretching exercises with Nicole, checked her blood pressure, and logged  her vital signs. After all this very necessary preliminary work, the moment Nicole had so eagerly anticipated finally arrived. Jeff came to get Nicole and escorted her to the tennis courts for her first 'official' lesson.

In her heightened state of awareness, Nicole took in everything. She smiled to herself as she enjoyed the piped-in music on the courts urging her to move to its rhythm. Even the yellow-green balls seemed so much more brilliant, and had so much more bounce than the used balls she was accustomed to practicing with.

"Who have you been working with?" Jeff asked. Who has been giving you lessons?"

Nicole told Jeff about Mr. Novak; the story of how they came to practice together.

"We help each other out!" Nicole cheerfully added.

"So you have never really *had any* formal lessons?" he asked.

Nicole sheepishly replied, "I guess you could say that!"

As they continued their baseline rally, Jeff was impressed with Nicole's level of play, her hustle. At one point, he stopped and called over to the next court.

"Bill—take a look at this twelve-year-old. She's something really special. She's never had any lessons. She's a real diamond in the rough."

As they continued, Jeff worked on what he called "a circuit of shots" to determine Nicole's skill on strokes— forehands, backhands, lobs, approach shots, volleys, overheads, and finally serves. He assessed her strengths, and more importantly determined where she needed stroke attention.

He finally asked Nicole a couple of questions. "Are you able to keep the ball deep most of the time? Have others been able to take advantage of your second serve?

It seemed that Jeff could read Nicole's mind. With some embarrassment she replied, "Jeff, the ability to keep the ball deep and a weak second serve, actually *are* the two areas that have hurt me the most all year."

"Together, we are going to refine your game and add to your arsenal of shots," he smiled. He then posed a challenge. "Nicole, you need to practice as if you are right in the heat of the competition. If you take risky shots, execute them with confidence; truly believe in yourself."

He continued, "Nicole, I'm noticing a vast improvement in your game, with the graphite racquet. You have so much better control. I encourage you to use it all the time now. The racquet has a much wider sweet spot; coupled with the size and the stringing tension, it also increases the speed of the return.

The three hours went by quickly. Nicole started to walk around and fetch the balls, piling them up on her racquet.

"Nicole, you don't have to pick up the balls. See that man over there?"

Nicole looked over to see a man driving a special vehicle to scoop up the balls.

In awe, "Wow!" was all Nicole could say.

They sat under a small canopy, providing shade from the sunny court. An employee wearing the designated club uniform, khaki shorts with a white polo shirt, rushed over to bring a variety of beverages— ice water with lemon, iced tea and fresh lemonade.

"Drink up. I hope you had fun and will come back tomorrow! What do you say? Are you up for it again tomorrow?" Jeff asked.

Nicole just laughed.

Jeff continued, "Seriously, Nicole, the level of play at the nationals is over the top. There is a lot of pressure. Players and parents aren't always on their best behavior. We only have twenty-three more practices to refine your game. You really jumped in head first today. I appreciate your hustle. But it's going to take hard work *every* day to get you ready to play at the national level."

"You don't have to worry about me. I love tennis. I appreciate all your help and I can assure you that I'll continue to work hard and give you my best every day!"

Jeff smiled. "That's what I thought. I'll see you tomorrow at 9:00. Oh—and if you want to bring your swimming suit, the kids all go in the pool after lunch."

At the gate, Mia was eagerly waiting. As Nicole approached she asked, "Well? How did it go?"

"Absolutely fantastic! I think I can better imagine what Beverly Hills must be like!"

That night over dinner Nicole shared the events of her day with her family. The level of detail in her development program amazed everyone.

Mia smiled. "Remember, God works in mysterious ways!" she winked.

Nicole was excited but again mentioned that it really seemed to be weird to be at the club without Erin. Carol informed everyone that she had successfully traded her off days with a colleague at work. She reminded everyone— this was her last week of vacation for this year. Everyone understood. This change in plans meant the family would have to forfeit this year's week at the lake. While Jon was looking forward to the lake vacation, he liked the idea of going to San Diego even more.

Mr. Nelson called. Nicole told him that everything at the club was better than she had ever dreamed or hoped for. He was pleased and told Nicole that he obtained SeaWorld tickets for the family.

"Nicole, I forgot to mention. I added your name as our guest. Please make sure that you eat lunch every day. Order any snacks or drinks you want. It takes a lot of energy. You need to eat well and stay hydrated. Just sign your name on the slip and it'll be put on my account. We want you to feel comfortable and enjoy yourself. After your lessons, stay as long as you like. Enjoy the pool and the rest of the facilities."

Nicole then called Mr. Novak and told him that she was participating in a very demanding and challenging tennis program. She informed him that she would be unable to hit with him until after the tournament.

"Nicole, I really understand. No problem, he replied and added, "Besides, I really wanted to take some time off to work on some projects around the house. I am so excited that you are going to the Nationals. I'm so proud of you. I know you'll do your best; that's all that counts, champ! Make sure you call me with weekly updates. I want to hear about everything!"

The next four weeks were amazing. Mia admired Nicole's dedication. She knew her granddaughter was very dedicated, and wouldn't miss a day. Nicole understood how fortunate she was to have been given this opportunity, and would make the most of it. Mia was convinced that Erin was smiling down on Nicole and encouraging her friend.

During the intensive training period, Nicole came to realize that she had gained six pounds of muscle. Could it be the Nautilus and her new diet? Mr. Lewis reinforced that she was making great progress in the strength training portion of her program. To date, she had increased her lifting weights twice and was starting to show muscle definition. Sally suggested some new stretching exercises, which Nicole incorporated into her original stretching regime based on Mr. Novak's suggestions. At home she demonstrated a few exercises to Jon and showed him the start of her "six-pack." One of the exercises, the "burpee," consisted of four positions: From a standing position and hands above your head you move to a squatting position with your palms on the floor. From there you assume a pushup position. Finally, you jump back up to the original position with your hands above your head. Nicole demonstrated the exercise, and Jon tried to follow along. Nicole told Jon that it was a great exercise to use as a warm up before playing basketball.

Mia began to prepare the foods Sally had recommended. The whole family, in fact, chose to incorporate the servings and recommendations of the "Food Pyramid" into their everyday eating. This was a healthy balanced diet which included— 6-11 daily breads or grain servings, focusing on healthier, whole-wheat; 3-5 vegetable servings which thankfully was no problem, since they all loved salads and most vegetables; at least 2-4 fruits, leaning towards fresh, in-season fruits and those high in vitamin C, like oranges; at least 2-3 glasses of milk, especially for the kids with growing bones; and 5-7 ounces of lean meat and protein such as chicken, turkey, and fish. While McDonald's was not out of the question, they would be 'challenged' to choose more carefully off its menu. Nicole was determined and decided, that she "could and *would* do it!" Carol loved the new focus on healthy eating. As a family, they had always tried to follow a relatively healthy diet, but this new emphasis on health was very timely for all of them.

Within the first few days of practice, Jeff noticed that Nicole's shoes although adequate, did not appear to be very supportive. He mentioned to Carol that good shoes were essential for optimal performance. As soon as Carol received her next paycheck, she purchased two pairs of K-Swiss tennis shoes to surprise Nicole.

One week quickly morphed into the next; Jeff and Nicole began to bond and to build trust. Jeff placed great emphasis on the mental game, suggested positive thinking and visualization of a positive outcome. Between points, he reminded Nicole to focus on her breathing, to slow her breathing down and return to a normal rhythm. He reinforced the need to remain centered; to find a way to remain calm whether a game was in her favor or her opponent's. He drilled Nicole hard, forcing her to execute proper, accurate shots, in an effort to promote self-confidence in her strategy and game. She began to play in her "zone," with heightened awareness along with increased focus and concentration.

Jeff coached Nicole to develop a 'total game' and encouraged her to become more offensive. Nicole's play became more aggressive and she started to attack whenever possible, requiring her to take more balls on the rise. He analyzed and broke down her strokes, then suggested changes which resulted in improved footwork and balance when setting up. He taught Nicole that relaxing her muscles rather than tightening them, would result in far greater power. They had lengthy discussions about the age-old tennis dilemma; power versus control. Everyone, it seems, gives one up for the other. However, a relaxed grip on the racquet allowed for power and control to work in harmony. He made a slight change to Nicole's grip (semi-Western, with the hand more around the racquet) and to the location of her toss on serve. He worked with Nicole, to better disguise her first and second serve by executing either from a consistent toss location. He stressed the need to propel her weight forward over the baseline after contact.

With practice, Nicole's first serve had more energy but much less spin, providing her with a greater opportunity to control the point from the start.

Jeff told Nicole, "Grip it and rip it!" as he worked with her to put more spin on her second serve. Within a short time, Nicole's serve had some great kick. Since Nicole had early-on identified her serve as the biggest concern, she felt very pleased.

From the baseline, they continued to work on keeping the

ball deep. "Most points are won after a dual of ground strokes from the baseline," he told her. She learned to employ more of a sitting position. He encouraged her to synchronize her stroke; to plant her front foot as she made contact with the ball, whenever possible. This would insure that her weight was continually moving forward as she stepped into the ball. Finally, he urged her to drop the racquet's head slightly just before contact, thereby adding more topspin and to accelerate the racquet's head through the ball to add power. After a solid hip rotation, she was encouraged to finish by following through, and momentarily holding her pose.

Jeff complimented Nicole on her backhand grip and stroke. "Whoever taught you your backhand really knew something about tennis. Who was it?"

"My Dad!"

Nicole smiled as she recalled her mom telling her that dad had been a fine all-around athlete. He played college basketball at the University of Wisconsin—Milwaukee; where her parents met.

All these positive changes, along with Erin's racquets elevated Nicole's basically good game, to another level. Using the added power and strength, Nicole and Jeff worked on inside-out forehands and backhands. He suggested other options for baseline play. He improved Nicole's drop shot by adding more disguise to it; a surprise tactic utilizing underspin. Jeff coached Nicole to prepare for a normal groundstroke, but to open up the racquet head just before contact, attempting to keep the ball on the strings just a bit longer. They worked on approach shots using both topspin and underspin. Jeff emphasized the advantage of using this shot in response to a piercing shot or an unforced short ball. It was the tactical shot to use when placement of the ball far outweighed velocity.

Nicole's net game also improved significantly. Her volleys were more accurate, utilizing more underspin and less pace. She learned to start a backhand volley with two hands and finish with one. Jeff showed her how to disguise topspin lobs from the baseline. Nicole practiced setting up for a passing shot, then suddenly dropped the racquet head, cut the ball in an upward motion, and followed through. This shot, as well as the drop shot, required greater mastery of touch. Overheads that once seemed such a challenge were no longer difficult as Nicole learned to run around the ball better and jump consistently off her back foot.

Four times a week, Nicole played matches with the boys, who provided solid competition. Initially uncomfortable playing the boys, once the matches were underway Nicole easily resumed her all-business "tennis mode." Within three weeks, she started to consistently beat all the boys except for Phillip, who was ranked fourteenth in the boys' sectional 16's. Oftentimes, Jeff would stand behind her and offer suggestions. On occasion he would even stop play if he thought his advice to be that important. His advice and guidance greatly aided Nicole's shot selection.

Jeff and Nicole drilled daily. They positioned themselves on the baseline in the doubles lanes and practiced forehands and backhands, keeping the ball deep and within the lanes. Since the net was much higher at this point, this drill required solid topspin and follow-through. Now that Nicole's first serve had become such a valuable weapon, she put new emphasis on her 'serve and volley' game. The three-ball drill was instrumental in her success. In this drill, Nicole hit a baseline shot and Jeff returned a short ball. Nicole hit a suitable approach shot and followed it in. Jeff then returned the ball for Nicole to volley appropriately. Nicole's positioning and timing improved as a direct result of this drill. As a result, Nicole's volley position more similarly resembled a two-foot jump stop (like she had learned from Coach Luebstorf in basketball), with a subsequent cross-step on the volley.

While Nicole had a great service return, Jeff also improved this aspect of her game, making this an even stronger weapon in her tennis arsenal. For practice, he stood at the service line and from this shorter distance hit her serves very quickly. This exercise improved her service 'blocking' technique by eliminating swings. Keeping her eyes focused on the ball, Nicole quickly learned to convert the power of her opponent's serve into her own power on the return. After this drill, returning serves from the standard distance seemed easy and almost effortless in comparison.

By the end of the fourth week, Nicole knew she was making great strides. With regularity, she now was hitting targets Jeff had posted at various points on the court. The target and situation drills proved to be valuable tools. This week, she achieved a personal record in the doubles lane drill; 43 forehands and 58 backhands in the doubles lanes in a row, all within two feet of the baseline. Additionally, her first serve regularly hit the backstop on one bounce, her second serve kicked over five feet, and her successful drop-shots had increased to 80%.

On her last day at the club, Nicole beat Phillip, 7-6, in a very competitive match. Crushing an inside-out forehand, she followed it in with a crisp volley to end the set.

Jeff was ecstatic. "Yes Nicole! Looks like the three-ball drill. You *are* ready for the big stage, young lady!" he called out.

Phillip was both shocked and impressed. He grinned, and wished Nicole luck.

Over the past few weeks, Jeff had worked very closely with Nicole and had grown very fond of her. He gave her a big hug and told her, "Nicole, I've never seen a more dedicated player. Your transformation over the past few weeks is nothing less than incredible. You've really made significant progress and I believe you will represent the Western Section very well at the Nationals."

Looking up, Nicole glimpsed Mr. Nelson who had been viewing the match from a distance. He smiled, and waved. She waved back.

All at once, Nicole realized the significance. This was her final practice at the club with Jeff.

She was the only player from the club going to a national tournament.

By this time, she had made some good friends at the club, getting to know many of them in the afternoons, when she stayed to swim and enjoy the club amenities after her morning practices. Today, they all gathered at the pool on this, her last day. They ate lunch, tanned and played. At the end of the afternoon, they wished Nicole the best of luck. Before leaving, Nicole handed a personal thank-you card to everyone who had helped her. She mailed a special card to the Nelsons, expressing her gratitude for their generous support.

That night, Carol hosted a party to thank everyone. Mia spent the entire day preparing everything for the celebration. The feast included a fresh veggie platter, hamburgers, Mia's home-made baby red potato salad, and cherry Jell-O with cherries. Nicole's favorite—angel-food cake with whipped cream mixed with fresh strawberries—was served for dessert. By 6:00 everyone arrived. Jeff came with his wife, and brought Phillip. The Stanwoods came, as did the Novaks. Carrie and Cindy appeared. The Nelsons stopped, but could not stay for dinner. Mrs. Nelson wasn't feeling well. It was a fun night. Everyone seemed to have a great time. Dr. Stanwood reminded Jon that the canoe would be waiting for him, whenever he could get out to the lake.

After everyone left, Nicole made a list of everything she would need for her trip. The family packed their suitcases. Tomorrow would be the day they had all looked forward to for so long.

**12**

# FOLLOW THROUGH
# AND FINISH YOUR SHOT

The entire Harris household was up early for breakfast and eager to be on their way to San Diego. On the way to the airport, they made a quick stop at St. Elizabeth's, where Nicole prayed for strength, and guidance. She lit candles in memory of her dad and Erin.

"Dad, thanks for always watching over me. I know you've been helping me prepare for this tournament. You taught me how to play tennis, Daddy. I know you were with us on the courts when Jeff was helping me. Sometimes, I could almost hear your voice when Jeff was coaching me. I love you so much! I miss you."

Next she thought about her dear friend, Erin. "Erin, I really wish you were still here. You deserve to be going to the nationals. I am so touched by your dad and mom's generosity and kindness. I am so grateful to your family, Erin. I know that you will be at my side. I hope and pray that I will do my best at the tournament and make you proud of me, Erin.

"Dad and Erin, I love you both!"

Finally, she ended saying the Lord's Prayer, asking for help to do her best.

Arriving at Mitchell Field on Milwaukee's south side was very exciting for Mia, Jon, and Nicole. Only Carol had ever flown before—on her honeymoon. Amid the roar of an aircraft as they approached, Jon commented, "I hope that we will be on a big plane."

"Why?" asked Nicole.

"To have enough room for all your new racquets!"

As they boarded, Jon was excited to catch a glimpse of the cockpit. Then luck really struck. The captain invited Jon into the cockpit and explained the purpose of all the instruments. Jon was so excited to see the instruments up close.

The flight was direct—four hours in the air. The family had seats in the middle of the plane, together in one row. Jon had the window. Nicole sat in the middle seat and Mia on the aisle. Carol had the other aisle seat across from Mia. Jon and Nicole were amazed to see Lake Michigan and other landmarks from the sky. The flight attendant, a very gracious woman, kindly explained exactly where they were at various times in the flight. The entire family, along with most of the other passengers, were in awe as they looked down upon the majestic Grand Canyon. The colors of the rock formations were truly breath-taking.

Everyone enjoyed the meal served on the plane. Jon liked the beverage cart and informed everyone the coke definitely tasted better than the ones in Milwaukee. Mia spent her time knitting almost the entire flight. Nicole and Carol read. Jon kept himself entertained with his Game Boy. Carol enjoyed chatting with the woman beside her. She was from Waukesha and going to visit her daughter in San Diego. "My daughter played tennis in high school," she mentioned to Carol. "There are a lot of tennis scholarships if you choose to stick with it," she added, and wished Nicole good luck.

The hours went by quickly. Overhead, the captain announced, "Ladies and Gentlemen, please keep your seatbelts fastened. We have begun our descent and will be landing in San Diego in about fifteen minutes."

Minutes later they heard the landing gear coming down. Carol commented, "I'm glad we didn't experience a lot of turbulence. It really was a smooth flight. I remember the flight that Rick and I took to Arizona. It felt like we were on a bumpy roller-coaster!"

The engines grew louder, as the runway came into sight. The plane made a smooth landing, swung around, and taxied toward the terminal. With anticipation building, the airplane door finally opened, after what seemed like a very long time. As they exited, they noticed the signs, Welcome to San Diego. They gathered their luggage and obtained their rental car; ready to start their San Diego adventure.

They drove out of the airport. True to California, it was a beautiful, sunny day. It was 11:00 in the morning, and already a perfect 84 degrees. Graceful palm trees lined the boulevards. Flowers were everywhere, scenting the air with a sweet, balmy fragrance.

"This is like heaven," said Mia.

The Nelsons had given them excellent directions. They traveled north on I-5 to the Morena Boulevard exit. The Hyatt was close to San Diego University, the site of the national tournament. Carol knew that this reservation was originally for the Nelsons, but she didn't mention it to the others. What an amazing gift from the Nelsons, she pensively reflected.

A sign appeared—SAN DIEGO UNIVERSITY—3 MILES—and Nicole started to get excited. They found the Hyatt, and pulled into the beautiful circular drive, lined by beautifully manicured lawn and palms. Eight huge pillars stood like sentinels; welcoming guests into the hotel. The main entrance doors were fifteen feet high. A valet came over to park the car, but Carol declined. She would check in and self-park the car, closer to their room.

The lobby was modern and spacious, with a huge counter and a concierge office. It was filled with many couches and chairs arranged into conversation areas. The hotel featured two restaurants, two swimming pools, an outdoor Jacuzzi, a game room, and a business/computer room. Outside was a putting green, and the hotel provided clubs and balls for checkout. As he gazed around, Jon's eyes got larger and larger. "Holy smokes, Nicole! Is this like Hollywood?" he asked.

She laughed. "Yeah. All we need is a map of the stars."

Carol and Mia checked-in and received a door card for each of them, along with a hotel map designating their room. Jon and Nicole were eager to see their room. They drove the car to the entrance nearest their room, parked, and unloaded. They spotted the pool which appeared to be very inviting. They were eager to try it out!

Checking the numbers, Carol stopped.

"Look at the number on the door," cried Nicole. "Suite 444!"

"Wow, I guess this *must* be our room!!" Mia exclaimed.

Yes, 4 had always been Nicole's favorite number, just like her Dad.

Inside was a comfortable living room, an ample eating

area with a microwave and small refrigerator, and two bedrooms, each with its own bathroom. Off the living room, a balcony overlooked the pool.

"This is a lot better than the Red Roof!" Jon remarked.

Everyone definitely was in awe. Each bedroom had two queen beds, so Jon and Nicole would share one room and Carol and Mia would share the other. It was already noon local time. Nicole was required to check in at USD; so she quickly changed. She hoped to meet Terry and hit for a while. Carol agreed to take Nicole, while Mia and Jon remained at the hotel. Already enjoyably resting in a high-back chair, Grandma picked up her needles and began to knit. Jon watched TV for a while, and then he and Mia decided to go for a dip in the pool.

On their way out, Carol and Nicole noticed the gift shop. "Can I please stop for a minute?" asked Nicole. "I want to send postcards to our friends back home!" Her list included Cindy, Carrie, Jeff, the Novaks, the Stanwoods, Nelsons and several others. In the lobby, they quickly wrote out the cards. Fifteen minutes later, they were in the mail.

The drive was gorgeous. The beautiful Spanish architecture was so different from the houses in Wisconsin. Mission Bay, and the view of the mesmerizing ocean, made Lake Michigan pale in comparison. A sign, THE UNIVERSITY OF SAN DIEGO, greeted them as they entered the school grounds. Officially "on campus," they followed the signs to the Tennis Center, where a large banner draped over the entrance read, WELCOME PLAYERS—THE GIRLS

14's NATIONAL HARDCOURT CHAMPIONSHIPS— 1989.

At the main desk three women signed in the players. Each handled names of a different segment of the alphabet. Nicole walked over to wait in the "A through H" line. Nicole signed in and received a hand-written note from Terry. She booked a court from 1:00 - 2:15 for them to warm up.

Nicole found a pay phone and called Terry's room to confirm. With a half hour left to spare, they checked out the courts and the draw. The University of San Diego, a member of the West Coast Conference, was proud of its state-of- the-art facilities—second to none. There were sixteen courts, four of which were stadium courts. All were currently filled with players. Most included tennis pros, who could be heard drilling and urging on younger players. Directives like "Out in front!" and "Finish!" were heard from a variety of voices. On occasion, a scream erupted as a girl missed an attempt.

They made their way to Court One. Just adjacent, a board some ten feet tall displayed the entire tournament draw. At the top, sixteen seeds from all over the United States were listed in numerical order. Nicole perused the seeds, and then looked in the main draw seeking her name.

"There I am, Mom!" she exclaimed, "Nicole Harris— Milwaukee, Wisconsin."

Nicole's first match was scheduled for Thursday, the day after tomorrow, the opening day of the tournament. At 9:00 a.m. she would play Katie Andrews from North Platte, Nebraska. If she won, Nicole noticed, she would not meet a seed until the third round. She felt extremely lucky. She found Terry's name and some of the girls from the Western Section. She pored over the doubles draw and was pleased to find the Smith twins seeded number two after winning the Western championship in Michigan. The singles seeding was as follows:

Singles

1. Andrea Phillips - Ventura, CA
2. Shannon Meyers - Las Vegas, NV
3. Jessica Rimmer - Kansas City, MO
4. Sara Luvell - Indianapolis, IN
5. Tanya Terrian - San Antonio, TX
6. Gail Evans - Miami, FL
7. Barb Luebstorf - Louisville, KY
8. Brenda Badad - Chicago, IL
9. Anita Rodriguez - Tallahassee, FL
10. Debby Thomas - Orlando, FL
11. Tayler Schommer - Buffalo, NY
12. Sue Parker - Memphis, TN
13. Jill St. John - Boston, MA
14. Sally Cavanaugh – Provo, UT
15. Abby Elkins - Sacramento, CA
16. Eve Kastenholtz - Pompano Beach, FL

Nicole went to stretch out on the grass. Carol continued to assess the draw. Soon Terry and her family arrived, and greeted Nicole and Carol with big smiles. It was nice, they said, to finally see familiar faces from the Midwest.

Terry and Nicole obtained a bucket of balls from the main

desk and made their way to their court. For Terry, this was also her first trip to the nationals. Both girls were clearly in awe of the magnitude of the facility and tournament itself. They hit a series of shots and then played some games. After about ten minutes Terry commented, "Nicole—you're hitting the ball much harder! And your strokes are really looking great!"

"Thanks Terry," said Nicole. "And you're as good as ever!"

Nicole was excited to win seven out of the eleven games they played, but she remained silent. I really have improved, she mused. The two spent their remaining time hitting serves. Both knew that serves were such a vital part of the game, often deciding a match.

With their allotted time up, they walked to the desk to reserve a court for 8:30 the next morning. It would be everyone's last practice day before the event. The families said their goodbyes and promised to meet at the court tomorrow.

Carol and Nicole hurried back to the hotel. Nicole wanted to spend time in the pool with Jon before cleaning up for the night. They had a great time, enjoying the cool, refreshing water. At 4:00 they went upstairs, cleaned up, and changed clothes. They had tickets for SeaWorld tonight and intended to have dinner there.

It took only twenty minutes to drive to Mission Bay and SeaWorld. Once there, they viewed more fish species than they ever knew existed. The "Dolphin Show" was fantastic.

Everyone in the audience enjoyed watching the dolphins perform to music. They grabbed a bite to eat, and made their way to the next "Shamu Show," the most enjoyable feature of all. Everyone was amazed to watch the whales obey the trainers' commands.

After the show, the Harrises stayed for the SeaWorld Beach Party. The audience sat in bleachers across a small body of water viewing a stage. Surfer, Beach Boy music that Nicole loved, played loudly, as surfers and water-skiers performed tricks. The show also showcased a clown—the designated fall-guy for the sketches. At the beginning of the performance, the emcee asked for volunteers to participate. Nicole stood up and raised her hand. The emcee roved through the crowd and chose eight individuals. Nicole was disappointed that she was not among those selected to assist. In fact, he walked past her, several times. As the show began, it became very obvious that those selected were in-fact specially-trained performers who performed in the skits every night of the week. At the end, the emcee introduced the 'volunteers' and shared with the audience their impressive background credentials. It proved to be a memorable night.

They drove slowly back to the Hyatt, taking in all the charm that night-time San Diego had to offer. By 10:00 everyone was ready to turn in, especially since it was really midnight according to the Harris family's biological clocks. Day One, was wonderful and now in the books.

The wake-up call came at 7:00 A.M. sharp. For breakfast they chose a restaurant overlooking the putting green.

Jon and Mia planned to do some golfing after Nicole and Carol left for the Tennis Center. They enjoyed a leisurely breakfast, and were on their way. On arrival, Nicole warmed up and stretched. When Terry arrived, they made their way to the court—a stadium court, which made the practice even more exciting. The girls had a vigorous practice. After they finished, both were ringing wet. Terry's first match was also scheduled for 9:00 tomorrow, so they agreed to meet at 8:00 to warm up together. Terry's family planned to spend the rest of the day at SeaWorld. Carol raved about the fun everyone had last night. She emphatically reminded everyone that Shamu was truly SeaWorld's star performer, but urged them to watch out for his splash.

Back at the Hyatt, Nicole and Carol joined Jon in the pool, as Mia sat nearby and knitted. By noon they were on their way to the San Diego Zoo at Balboa Park. There they enjoyed lunch and visited the exhibits. One of the highlights was the zoo tram, which gave everyone an incredible bird's-eye view of the entire complex from one side to the other. Worried about falling off into a cage, Jon clung to the side for safety.

By 3:00 everyone started to feel the effects from the heat. They decided to cool off and opted for refreshing, ice-cold snow cones, as they made their way to the exit. Although they didn't see the entire zoo, they saw most of it. Jon's favorite exhibit was the monkeys. Nicole's was the giraffes. Mia noticed Nicole appeared to be pensive, deep in thought. Mia knew her granddaughter well. Although Nicole appeared to be enjoying the zoo, she most likely was thinking about the tournament, the real reason why the family was here in San Diego today. So much contrast, Mia mused. A twelve year old so lighthearted and having fun, as young girls do—versus the pressure of a national tennis tournament!

They headed back to the hotel. They would need some time to prepare for the National Tennis Banquet which was scheduled for 6:00 in the student union ballroom. This mandatory tournament event was sponsored by Penn Corporation for the players and their families. The Harrises arrived fifteen minutes early and made their way through the lobby, filled with players and families. Vendors lined the perimeter of the room sitting at tables with colorful displays. They eagerly marketed the services they had to offer, similar to the compu-tennis in Michigan. When approached, Carol declined and continued through the crowd. Over the crowd noise, a loud, boisterous voice erupted—"Make way for the Florida Wrecking Crew! Here comes the Florida Wrecking Crew!"

A burly man accompanied by eight girls entered the lobby, each proudly wearing a T-shirt reading "The Florida Wrecking Crew." Florida had by far the largest contingency of any state—eight girls, with four boasting tournament seeding.

The crowd entered the banquet room. Large paper tennis balls hung from the ceiling. Tables were set for twelve, and everyone had an assigned seat. A hostess took the Harrises to their table. Nicole spotted Terry and her family in the corner and waved. As they made their way they heard, "On Wisconsin, On Wisconsin!" The Smith family stood and waved.

Joining them at their table was the Parker family from Tennessee. Sue was the twelfth seed. Rounding out the table were Dawn Evers and her parents from Mobile, Alabama.

Introductions were made.

"You sure talk funny!" Jon blurted out to Sue and Dawn.

Carol scolded him. Jon apologized, and everyone shared a chuckle.

With most of the seats filled, the emcee strutted out onto the stage. Above him and the podium a large sign read WELCOME—JUNIOR NATIONAL 14's GIRLS. He asked for everyone's attention, and the evening formally began. He introduced himself as Jimmy Monners, and told everyone, "But don't mix me up with Jimmy Connors. The only thing we have in common is that we're both left-handed." He smiled, and went on. "I'd like to welcome you all to the 1989 Junior 14's National Hard-court Championship sponsored by the United States Tennis Association and Penn Corporation."

After a few more brief comments, he added, "Let's all take a moment. Please bow your head and remember all of your blessings."

After a brief pause, he concluded, "Enjoy your dinner. I'll be back in about forty-five minutes."

Everyone ate heartily, as the entrée of Mongolian beef, broccoli and white rice was light but plentiful. Cake with ice cream completed the great meal. Both Mia and Carol enjoyed a cup of coffee along with their dessert to end the tasty meal. During dinner, they both noticed Nicole discretely glancing over observing Andrea Phillips, last year's winner, seated only a few tables away.

When everyone finished their dessert, Mr. Monners returned and made the announcement,

"All entrants please pick up your packets and tournament T-shirts in the back of the room at the end of the night. They are listed alphabetically, left to right."

He next introduced Pam Sullivan, the tournament director, who welcomed the girls and their families and explained the rules and conduct of the tournament. As she spoke, several others could be heard mumbling, not paying attention.

Mrs. Sullivan concluded by wishing everyone good luck. Mr. Monners returned; microphone in hand, to introduce the guest speaker. "We have a special surprise —a bit of entertainment in the form of Ted Trambler, a local comedian and Rodney Dangerfield impersonator." With that he yelled, "Heeerrrre's TED."

Mr. Trambler ran onto the stage and started his monologue. His jokes, at first flat, soon grew on the crowd. His puns included "no strings attached," "*what* a racquet," "this must be over *your* heads—get it, overheads?," "serve *this* up," "net wit," "hey, *net*compoop," and "can you match that?" Most of his puns elicited groans, but he continued. "Don't like 'em, huh? One tough crowd, I tell ya! Must be the *group*!! Couldn't tell if the dinner was Chinese food or beef steak—talk about *moo* goo gai pan? Or was it *bed* pan?" He bugged his eyes, got a huge laugh, and grinned. "Hey, I'm on a roll—an *egg* roll? He peeked at his shoes. "Uh, right," he said. The laughs came, louder. "I can't believe all you young girls play tennis so well! When I was thirteen, I was playing marbles. When I was fourteen and I saw a cute girl, I just about lost my marbles!"

At this point, he clearly won over the crowd, who now responded with roaring laughter. "Best match *I* ever saw? Wasn't Martina and Chris in the finals. No—it was me and Superman!" At this, some of the parents rolled their eyes, but most loved it and laughed. Even Mia smirked.

"Yup, last time I was courtside I fought to win, too—but, my wife and her lawyer took it all—game, set, match! Well, time to get back to McDonald's for the night shift? I tell ya!"

He bowed, and stomped off the stage, rolling his bug-eyes as only he could do.

Mr. Monners returned to the stage and announced that the night would conclude with a raffle drawing. Each seat had been assigned a number. The first lucky winner would receive an autographed tape of Mr. Trambler's Greatest Jokes. Second-place would receive *two* autographed tapes!" he announced.

Mia and the others burst into laughter. After the first winner was announced, he called out a familiar name. Terry's mother was the second lucky raffle winner. As the evening ended, Mr. Monners reminded everyone to have fun and wished all the girls good luck.

In the back of the room, Mr. Trambler sat at a table, hoping to sell his tapes. A young woman assisted him.

"Boy, what a racquet *that* is," said Mia.

"Gram—you made a joke!!"

They all laughed. Nicole got up and got into the line for her packet. Within minutes, the room was empty.

The drive home was beautiful, very relaxing. A full moon hovered in the sky. It had been a wonderful day. San Diego, Day Two, was but a memory. Within a few short hours, the eagerly anticipated first day of the national tournament, would be here. Nicole wished she could see the future, and wondered what tomorrow would bring. Yes, the tournament *was* the reason they were here. Now it was up to her. Since May she had worked very hard, but in her wildest dreams never thought this moment would come this year. The next four days would determine her fate. It was time to dig down deeply and capture the moment.

The Harrises got to bed early. Although none of them discussed it, they each knew that the fun was over. The time to demonstrate on the court what she had daily practiced had come. As Nicole and Jon got in their beds, Jon murmured, "Sis, don't worry. You'll be great."

"Thanks, Jon, I love you" she whispered, as they both fell into a deep, restful sleep.

## 13

**HOLD YOUR POSE**

E arly the next morning Carol knocked on the bedroom door.

"Nicole and Jon—rise and shine!"

She opened the door, to two sleepy voices—"Morning, Mom..."

Nicole climbed out of bed and headed to the bathroom to get dressed. Jon did likewise. Mia had been up for an hour. She came in and presented Nicole with a soft cotton headband she knitted. On it, Nicole noticed her initials "NH." Nicole gave Mia a big hug.

"I love it Gram! It will be my lucky headband!"

After Nicole finished her stretching exercises, they were ready to leave. Once again, Jon chose the restaurant overlooking the putting green. Eight other tennis families were already eating. Breakfast came quickly and was delicious.

By 7:40, they were on their way. The facility was buzzing with families, players, and pros. A Compu-tennis representative approached. "No, thank you," Mia said, quickly. Many offered printout information on each girl. People openly dropped tennis names, not caring who was present. The Florida Wrecking Crew made its entrance, led by the same man as the night before. He pointed to his FLORIDA WRECKING CREW shirt and announced, "Folks, they're here! The wrecking crew has arrived!"

Surprisingly, Mr. Nelson came by. He came to support the Wisconsin contingency. He asked the Harrises if their accommodations were okay. Carol told him that everything was wonderful and thanked him. He noticed Nicole in her headband, and quipped—"Who is she? Jim McMahon?"

They laughed. "We decided to spice things up, since she's not on the computer of veteran players," said Mia. "This way everyone will know who she is.

He laughed. "Well, regardless, I just wanted to wish you the best of luck, Nicole. And by the way, Mrs. Nelson and I both enjoyed the thoughtful thank-you postcard."

"I really appreciate all you've done for me. I hope I can live up to your expectations."

"You're most welcome, young lady! My only expectation is for you to have fun and play your best. No matter the outcome, I'll be happy and always proud of you."

He gave her a pat on the back, and departed. Terry and her family appeared, and told Nicole, to insure that everyone got practice time, only fifteen-minute blocks of practice time were available. They had secured a court from 8:15 until 8:30, so they had to hurry.

Terry already had the balls, so she and Nicole made their way down the path to Court Seven. With officials monitoring, the previous group came off the court punctually, allowing Terry and Nicole to warm up, practice their strokes, and work up a solid sweat in the allotted time. About halfway through the warm-up, Nicole looked over at the next court and saw Andrea Phillips. For a moment, Nicole stood in awe.

She experienced a flashback, and once again re-lived watching Andrea win the tournament on television last summer. As Nicole watched, Andrea made a few errors that were quickly corrected by her tennis pro. Nicole's fears seemed to fall away. "Do you know who that is?" asked Terry, as they left the court. "I sure do," answered Nicole.

"The number-one seed!"

Already 8:30, the two headed back to the main desk to join their parents. A crowd had convened on the grass, most wearing athletic warm-ups with school names and logos.

"Coaches, scouting talent for colleges," explained Terry.

Nicole noticed coaches from Boise State, Pepperdine, USC, Stetson, Texas, Wisconsin, NAU, and Oregon. "I was hoping to see the coach from ASU—that's Arizona State University. Many people say she's just incredible. She gets the most out of her players, but is kind and mother-like. She pushes the student-athlete concept to the hilt. All of her players graduate on time.

"Sounds great," said Nicole.

"She is. Everyone wants to play for her."

At the desk they joined their parents and found a place to sit. Precisely at 9:00 came the announcement—"Williams, Bronson." Terry jumped up, ready. Nicole stepped over and wished her luck.

After three more calls, it was Nicole's turn. "Andrews, Harris."

Nicole stood up, took a deep breath, looked at her family, and smiled. The time she had dreamed about had arrived. Even though she had to go onto the court alone, her support group was right there. She had worked very hard for the last five weeks. She had dramatically improved every facet of her game, but would it prove to be enough? How would her game stack up against the top junior players in the United States?

Mia, Carol, and Jon gave her hugs and kisses and wished her luck. At the desk, she met Katie Andrews. She shook her hand, introduced herself, and received the two allocated balls from the director. As she walked by, she flashed the balls to her family—Penn 4's. She smiled.

Both sets of parents followed the girls out. Most courts had bleachers for viewing. But, with the sun already hot and the sky cloudless, there was no protection. Everyone was wearing a hat and sunglasses. Regardless, this inconvenience was a small price to pay to watch your daughter, sister, or granddaughter compete in this prestigious tennis competition.

Officials roved around the courts as play began, watching for foot-faults and bad line calls. They had the authority to make or overturn a call on the spot. Their role was to handle disputes and serve as line judges, staying as long as necessary on any court, until the match or disagreement was under control.

Katie and Nicole placed their gear on the bench and took the court. Nicole was using Erin's racquet as she took her position. She had practiced with it for long hours, and it had made a huge difference in terms of power and control. The girls began with ground strokes, then each made her way to the net to volley and hit overheads. Finally, each took some serves, finishing just before the ten-minute requirement. They made their way to the bench for a quick drink of water.

"Okay, ladies? Let's get this match started!" announced the official.

Nicole wished Katie good luck and spun her racquet. Seeing the "E.N" prominently displayed on the handle, Nicole won the right to choose, and opted to serve first. Just before Nicole stepped out to start the match, she paused and looked into the stands for her family. She saw them, smiled, nodded, and with new determination headed to the baseline. Arriving on the baseline, she was ready for her formal introduction into national tournament play.

Nicole took a deep breath, as she threw up her first toss. The racquet caught the ball firmly, sending it just over the top of the net and skipping long over the service box, just missing Katie. Nicole sighed, and steadied herself. Again she tossed the ball, but her new motion cut across the ball and created extra spin and arch. The ball landed just past the middle of the box, and kicked wide to Katie's forehand. Katie lunged to hit the ball on the rise. Her effort sent the ball into the net; 15-love.

Nicole was pleased, and exhaled out loud. To date, she had never experienced such an easy point on her second serve, especially against such a seasoned opponent. She felt a renewed confidence in her serve today. Even if she missed her first serve, she was convinced that her second serve would not be easily exploited. She lined up, and served. Katie returned it to her backhand. Nicole quickly moved over, set her feet, and stepped into the ball while pointing her right foot down the line. She nailed the shot down the line that landed less than a foot from the baseline. Katie pursued, but barely got a racquet on the ball. In prior matches Nicole would never have tried that shot, especially this early in a match. But now she experienced a newfound confidence, thanks to her new racquet and the many hours of coaching she had received this last month. Nicole was pumped, and ready to try anything and everything.

As she lined up, she hesitated for just a second, her heart beating faster. Katie was moving back and forth, spinning her racquet, in her intensity to gauge Nicole's next serve. The serve came—again, right on the money—but this time Katie was able to return the ball. After a back-and-forth series of some eight baseline shots, Katie put up a short ball. Recognizing the opportunity, Nicole sprinted up and using top-spin, hit the ball hard and deep to Katie's backhand. Katie ran the shot down in the corner, but was only able to return an off-balance lob. Nicole stepped back, pointed at the ball with her left hand, set her feet, and then delivered a smooth overhead that bounced high over Katie's head; 40-love.

Nicole lined up, and with renewed energy served—a rocket. The ball hit on Katie's backhand side and spun towards her body. Its sheer speed handcuffed Katie, leaving her unable to swing. The ball caught the handle of Katie's racquet and bounced away.

Nicole won the first four points, taking the first game. The girls changed sides. As they passed, Nicole handed Katie the balls with "Here you go, Katie." Katie silently swiped the balls from Nicole's hand, and stalked towards the baseline. "I must be ready", Nicole thought, as her opponent appeared resolved to step up her game.

Katie's first serve was in. Nicole blocked it beautifully, to the deep back center of the court. Katie ran around the ball, hitting the return to Nicole's forehand. Nicole scampered over, set herself, pointed her left foot, and delivered a crisp return down the line for a winner. She was playing like she never had before!

As the match progressed, balls continued to come off Nicole's racquet with power and accuracy. Her confidence was building. She was making shots that only a month ago would have been wishful thinking. Yes, she had worked hard, but she also seemed to have a better understanding of the game. She was using the right shot, calculating percentages, and did not feel so rushed. Although Katie was not seeded, playing this well in a national tournament felt great.

Nicole did not let up, and led 5-1, with only four unforced errors. Then Katie surged and took the next two games, breaking Nicole's serve. Nicole gathered herself and created her own surge. She took the next four games, to give her the first set, 6-3, and a 3-0 second-set lead. Katie fought back, refusing to give up. She won the next game and appeared determined to get to the net, no matter what the circumstance. Even when the ball was not short, she took chances, racing in to change the game and pressure Nicole to hit around or over her. The tactic brought some initial success, however Nicole responded with some fine passing shots and topspin lobs.

At times, Nicole felt like she was doing a drill, just as she had practiced daily with Jeff at the net. After hitting the first few winners past Katie, Nicole realized she was relaxing her grip, and not tightening her muscles. With a flood of recall, she vividly remembered Jeff telling her the power would be there, if she relaxed her muscles. With Nicole up 5-1, it was Katie's serve. She blasted her serve to the inside part of the service box—an ace; 15-love. Nicole retrieved the ball, sending it back to Katie. She knew that she must rise to the occasion. She couldn't let Katie back into the match. Bent in her ready position, Nicole took a short, two-foot hop when Katie served the ball. Jeff explained that this movement would help her react quickly in either direction. It was an easy tip to remember—the same principle as approaching an offensive player on the move in basketball.

Katie hit another bullet. Nicole blocked the ball smoothly, sending it back deep to Katie's backhand side, using the power of Katie's serve to her own advantage. With the return better than she anticipated, Nicole followed it in. In haste, Katie returned a running backhand down the line. As the ball crossed the net, Nicole met it with a perfect volley to the opposite corner—a winner. Not often had Nicole come in on a service return. All the lessons seemed to have taken hold, and Nicole was now playing on auto-pilot.

The next two points came down to who would make the first error, and hit the short ball. Each girl did. At 30-30, Katie doubled-faulted, her first of the match. It was match point. Katie's next offering was long. Nicole readied herself for the second serve. The ball hit far back in the box and kicked deeper than normal. Nicole lunged, and hit the ball back just past the service line. Katie attacked with a topspin approach shot to the corner. As Nicole raced back, Katie moved up into her spot just inside the service line. Forced to hit on the run, Nicole offered a topspin lob to the opposite corner. The ball cleared Katie's outstretched racquet by a few feet and hit the corner of the court, kicking toward the screen.

Nicole hit a winner to win her first match, 6-3, 6-1. An elated Nicole approached the net, trying to contain her joy. She could sense Katie's sadness, losing the opening round of this important tournament. They shook hands.

"Nice match, Katie. Good luck in your next one," Nicole offered.

"Thanks, you, too." Katie replied.

On the way to the main desk they passed the stands. Nicole smiled at her family. Carol and Mia smiled back. Jon stuck his hand out to give a high five.

The girls reported the score and received their next assignments. With the double-elimination protocol, Katie was still in the tournament and could still finish as high as fifth place. Nicole would next face Amanda Cotton from Denver, Colorado, who moments ago won her match 6-0, 6-2 over Stephanie Marks from Eugene, Oregon. The match was set for 3:00. While Terry lost in straight sets 6-1, 6-3, top-seeded Andrea Phillips had won easily, 6-0, 6-0.

As the Harrises walked to the car, Carol and Mia told Nicole how well she played. "Some of your shots—amazing!"

they chimed in unison.

Nicole smiled. "Thanks. I couldn't believe some of them myself."

Back at the Hyatt, Nicole took a quick shower. She was refreshed, and felt so much better. It was 11:30. In about an hour they would have lunch. They rested in their living room and discussed the match. Nicole reminded everyone that Katie was not seeded, and the competition would spike very soon. Nicole and Carol kept glancing over at Mia. They were concerned because she seemed very hot and her face was bright red. Mia insisted she was fine, her face didn't hurt. Then Mia took off her sunglasses. While her face was flaming red, the spot where the glasses had covered was normal. "Gosh, Gram!" said Jon. "You look like a raccoon!" They all laughed.

Carol applied a cold compress to Mia's face and neck to cool her off. After a short time they went to lunch at the café overlooking the pool. They had heard the food was great but had not yet had the chance to taste it.

The food lived up to its reputation. While eating, they noticed several families enjoying themselves in the pool. They unanimously agreed, as soon as Nicole's next match was over, they would come straight back and cool off in the pool together.

After lunch, they found a shady spot to relax. At 2:00 Nicole went up to the room to get ready and stretch. At 2:15 they headed back to the Tennis Center, where they scanned the draw. Chuckling amazed, Mia said, "My goodness, all eight girls from the 'Wrecking Crew' have won their first matches!" The main draw had been reduced to 64. The next round would decrease the draw to 32. Nicole noted that Terry's next match was scheduled for 5 p.m.

A short distance away was Lucy Evans from Tucson, Arizona. "Hi Lucy," Nicole called. "Remember we played in Waukesha earlier this summer?"

"I sure do. Hi, Nicole."

"How are you doing?" asked Nicole.

"Not great, I lost this morning to one of the Florida girls, 0 and 2."

The call came for Lucy's match. "Nicole, I have to go. Let's talk later."

"Sure. Good luck in your next match Lucy. You'll do fine."

The doubles tournament would start later today, Nicole noticed. The Smith girls would play their first match.

Nicole retied her shoes and took a few loose practice swings with her racquet. She wanted to be ready when she heard her name called. At 3:10 the call came, "Cotton, Harris."

Mia, Carol, and Jon each gave Nicole a hug and she was on her way. Amanda was already at the desk, an extremely tall girl—at least six feet—with long brown hair and freckles. Being tall in her own right, it seemed strange for Nicole to look up at her opponent. She shook Amanda's hand and said, "Hello."

Amanda had the balls, so they walked to Court 16, at

the far end. Nicole noticed a large shade tree just next to the court—a perfect place for Mia, completely out of the sun. She waved to her family, pointing to the tree. They smiled and nodded. Nicole asked Amanda if her family was present. "No," she replied. "They're in Europe this summer. I'm here with my pro."

As they walked out to warm up, for a moment Nicole felt like she was about to play Mr. Novak, as Amanda was about the same height. The warm-up was very rigorous. Amanda hustled for every ball, and strived to win every point. Nicole thought this was a strategy aimed at breaking her confidence. After the warm-up, Amanda asked if they could play two more points. "Sure," answered Nicole. Amanda served a second serve. After six baseline shots, Nicole hit a winner up the line. Nicole served, also a second serve. Amanda powered the ball back, but into the net. She turned in frustration and walked back to the bench for some water. Nicole met her, and spun her racquet. Nicole won the spin.

The girls took their spots, ready to play. As Nicole lined up, Amanda moved back and forth, in and out, preparing to receive serve. Nicole's first offering was long. Nicole hit her second serve with much more spin, hoping it would kick and rise quickly. Amanda returned the ball deep to Nicole's forehand. Nicole ran over and hit it cross-court to Amanda's forehand. She responded with a shot down the line, and followed the ball in. Nicole quickly moved over; set her feet, delivering a backhand across court. Nicole shortened and accelerated her swing forcing the ball to fall short at

Amanda's feet on her backhand side. Amanda stuck out her racquet for an underspin backhand volley, but the ball skimmed under her racquet for Nicole's point.

Nicole's next serve was sent sharply back at her. She jumped to avoid being hit but at the same time extended her racquet. The ball came off Nicole's racquet high and short, landing on Amanda's side. Amanda followed her shot and was now in position to take control. She set her feet, and smashed the ball into the corner of Nicole's court. It bounced over the backstop and into the adjacent court.

With an apology, Nicole retrieved the ball from the adjacent court, where the players were forced to stop their match. As Nicole lined up, Amanda continued to move side to side, anticipating. Nicole took a deep breath, and hit a rocket to the inside of the service box toward Amanda's backhand. Amanda was unable to hit the ball as it bounced back to the screen—an ace. At 30-15, Nicole lined up, and hit another ace to Amanda's backhand. Nicole couldn't believe her power; her new serve was working wonders!

Amanda returned Nicole's next offering deep to her forehand. Nicole set herself, and hit the ball across court. Amanda answered with a baseline shot down the line and came in as Nicole scampered over. Unable to set her feet, Nicole hit a topspin lob to the opposite corner high over Amanda's considerable wingspan. The ball cleared, and bounced into the corner for a winner. As they changed sides, Amanda told Nicole that the sun impeded her view of that shot.

Amanda's serve was not particularly fast, but her height gave it more angle and a higher bounce, so Nicole retreated to return them. She assumed that Amanda would be running in with her serve and volley game. While Amanda approached with most of her first serves, she stayed back on her second. She seemed to have a knack for *knowing* where Nicole's return was headed. She volleyed her first two serves for winners, but Nicole's next return slipped under Amanda's racquet for a point.

Nicole knew that she would have to hit more shots like she did in game one, short and bouncing, at the feet of the charging Amanda. She would also have to add a few topspin lobs and—if she got an opening—a crisp passing shot. It would require an assortment of shots to combat such an aggressive opponent.

After Amanda won several points early on her serve, the girls went into game five knotted at 2-2. Each girl was holding serve. If they hit from the baseline, Nicole felt she had a solid chance of winning each point. Additionally, Nicole realized that the power and trajectory of Amanda's serve provided a perfect opportunity to rush the net. She remembered Jeff reviewing that scenario with her. His advice was simple and effective. "Move up and take the ball on the rise."

Nicole did so, and was able to put more pressure on Amanda and kept her off balance. After another shot slipped under the charging Amanda's racquet, Nicole broke Amanda's serve for the first time.

As they switched sides, Nicole hoped to break Amanda's

serve one more time. If so, the first set would be hers. She recalled Jeff's perspective. "Often all it takes to win a match is to break your opponent two or three times."

Although Nicole did not break Amanda again the first set, once turned out to be enough.

Nicole claimed the first set, 6-4. Nicole knew the match was far from over and she *must* keep the pressure on Amanda.

Nicole intended to start the second set strong. She won the first game, but was unable to break Amanda in the second. Down 3-4, Amanda opened with a double fault, her first. Then she missed a first serve. On her second, Nicole responded with a solid return at her feet. Amanda managed to scoop the ball over the net, but it landed short. Nicole sprinted in, and let the ball bounce. Amanda's only chance was to rush the net and cover as best she could. As she watched her opponent advance, Nicole took the ball off the bounce and lofted it deep into the opposite corner. With no chance, Amanda shrugged her shoulders and walked back.

Nicole recalled Jeff's insight. "Sometimes a big point can change the entire momentum of a match." If true, this definitely qualified as a big point!

Amanda then double-faulted. Nicole hit a powerful forehand off her subsequent serve and won the game. She was up 5-3. She only needed to hold serve to win the match.

Amanda refused to fold. She approached the net behind her service return, and the game went to deuce. Then Nicole delivered a crisp serve that Amanda returned short. Nicole ran up, set her feet, and smashed a winner. It was match point. Nicole took a deep breath, set up, met the ball perfectly, and smashed it to the outside of the service line to Amanda's backhand. Amanda could only watch the ball whiz past. For a moment, she simply stood. Finally, she lifted her hand in a flat parallel position to signify the shot was good, and made her way to the net.

Nicole trotted up to join her. The two shook hands. At the bench they gathered their gear and returned to the main desk to report the score.

Nicole added, "Good luck, Amanda,"

"Same to you." Amanda responded.

Carol, Mia, and Jon were all smiles and warmly embraced Nicole. They all agreed that she had played very well against a strong opponent. With many matches ongoing or yet to be played, they decided to come back later to review the draw and determine Nicole's next opponent. Maybe they would catch some of Terry's match, which was slated for 5:00.

As they had agreed at lunch, they were all eager to go swimming and down the water slide. So back at the motel, they enjoyed a wonderful hour in the pool. Nicole felt far more relaxed. They changed and headed back to the tournament.

Their first task was to check the draw. Terry's score was not listed—the match was still in progress—but the score of her next opponent was there. "All the members of the Florida Wrecking Crew won their matches *again*!!" Mia emphasized.

"I know, Gram. I'll be playing the top ranked crew

member—Gail Evans—at 9:00."

Gail already finished, winning 6-0, 6-1. Nicole was disappointed she did not have an opportunity to see her play. Rumor had it; she was off the court in under an hour. It was hard to believe.

"Don't forget to bring your hard hat," Mia laughed.

"Ha, ha Mia," Nicole replied.

"Nicole, I can't believe you've made it to the round of 32! I'm so proud of you!" Carol beamed with pride.

"Thanks, Mom."

Over at Terry's match, Nicole spotted Terry's mom, and learned the two girls had split sets.

Terry was up 4-2 in the third. Terry spotted Nicole, flashed a smile, and then went back to work. Her opponent, from Alaska, preferred to stay on the baseline. Each point took several hits. Finally, Terry finished strong, winning the last two games.

Nicole congratulated her. Although Terry was in the back draw, every win helped to improve her final national ranking and impress the college scouts. She would be a sophomore next year. Hopefully, a scholarship was on the horizon. Back at the desk, Terry and Nicole said goodbye. They agreed to warm up at 8:30 tomorrow, since they would both play at 9:00.

Back at the hotel Jon was given the task of choosing where to eat dinner.

"At the 'swimming pool restaurant'!"

Everyone laughed and knew exactly which restaurant Jon

had chosen. After a delicious dinner, they enjoyed frozen fruit bars at the pool. They sat and appreciated the beautiful night with a slight breeze, a star-filled sky, and reflected. Nicole understood the magnitude and importance of her next match. If she won, she would take a sixth seed's place. She *had* to bring her "A" game.

They watched some TV, and decided to retire early. Nicole needed to be at one-hundred percent, ready to go. Tomorrow might bring the biggest match of her life.

# QUICKLY GET BACK
# TO THE MIDDLE

The Harrises were up by 7:00 a.m., completed their morning rituals, and finished breakfast by 7:30. It was another beautiful, cloudless day. Nicole was quiet and pensive. Carol and Mia knew her mind was elsewhere. Taking Mom's suggestion, Nicole had eggs, whole-wheat toast, and fruit to provide a solid combination of carbohydrates and protein for energy and stamina. Nicole finished eating first and returned to the room to stretch.

Soon after, the others joined her, and together they left for the Tennis Center. The draw exhibited no surprises. All the seeds continued to win. Terry arrived, and she and Nicole warmed-up for fifteen minutes. They both hit extremely well, seldom missing a shot, even though it was only practice. By 8:30 both were ready.

Terry's next opponent was to be Lilly Mullins from Boston, Massachusetts. As they waited for their court times, Nicole and Terry wandered past Court Three. There, four girls clad in "Florida Wrecking Crew" shirts were hitting with a pro giving instructions. This was part of the infamous group from Florida drawing so much attention. Nicole noticed their leader, a burly, bearded man with a white sun hat seated beneath a broad umbrella and sipping coffee, enjoying the scene. One of these girls must be Gail Evans, but Nicole was clueless as to which one she was.

Soon Terry heard her name. Nicole and Terry wished each other luck. They decided to catch up and chat after the matches. Then "Evans, Harris" was announced. Nicole's heart thumped wildly as she hurried back to the desk. There she finally set her eyes on Gail Evans, the sixth seed and highest-ranked girl from Florida. Nicole was surprised. Gail was small, about 5'3," and very slender. While Nicole shook her hand, she did not seem friendly. As they made their way to the stadium court, Nicole asked, "Do you enjoy living in Florida?"

The staccato-like reply—"whatever!"

They placed their equipment next to the bench and began to warm up. Nicole noticed a group of coaches walk over to join the already sizeable and growing crowd for the match. Several Florida team members were on hand, along with their burly leader sipping on his morning coffee. Nicole spotted her family, stationed only a short distance away.

The impressive Stadium Court was a thrill for Nicole. This was the first time she had ever played in such a high-profile setting. The biggest crowd at any of her matches had been in Kohler against Erin. As the two warmed up, Nicole noticed Gail's proficiency and quickness from the baseline. Her agility, too, was readily apparent, as she easily reached every ball and returned each with ease. After only a few volleys and serves, Nicole was surprised to hear—"Are you ready?" Yes, she nodded. For she, too, felt warmed-up and eager to start.

At the net, Nicole proceeded to spin her racquet. Gail won, and elected to serve. Each returned to her bench for a quick drink of water, before proceeding to their positions on the baseline. Nicole glanced over. Her family smiled. Carol gave a thumbs-up. Mia offered a wink. Jon clapped, and shouted "Let's go, Nic!"

Nicole took a deep breath and shuffled her feet to prepare. Gail's first serve hit deep in the box. Nicole turned her body and hit a forehand back across court. Gail easily reached it and hit a rope down the line. Nicole answered with a running backhand, again across the court. Gail caught up and hit a powerful backhand down the line. Nicole barely got her racquet on the ball, and deflected it out of bounds. "Yes!" Gail screamed, as the ball settled against the fencing.

Gail stepped sternly back to the baseline. Her serve again was in, and Nicole returned it sharply. A new baseline rally ensued—shot after shot, each landing only a short distance from the end lines. After about a dozen shots, Gail hit a winner down the line. "Yes!" she yelled. Nicole was surprised, and quite disgusted with Gail's lack of sportsmanship. Nicole had never seen such a display of misbehavior from any of the great players such as Erin and others from the Westerns. Was this a "Florida thing"? Nonetheless, she decided, she had to deal with it; the sooner the better. Nicole decided to let her own game do the talking and put Gail's antics out of her mind, just as she had at Kohler when Angie Martin had started her stall.

Nicole's heart started to beat faster. Again the serve came, right on the money. Nicole stepped into the shot, and hit a blistering return. Gail had no time to even get racquet on the ball as it sailed by her feet.

Gail gave Nicole a half-angry look and retrieved the ball. Her next offering came, and once again Nicole crushed the return. As Gail hit her first short shot, Nicole rushed in, set herself, and, as the ball rose, hit a smooth groundstroke away for a winner; 30-30. Gail didn't look happy.

The next two points were lengthy skirmishes involving exceptional shots from each baseline. Neither player would give in. The first point ended when Nicole's shot hit the top of the net and drifted long. On the second, Nicole's shot was wide right. Pleased with her 1-0 start, Gail exclaimed, "Yes!" and smashed the remaining ball in her hand directly into the net.

As the match continued, the strength of Gail's baseline game became increasingly apparent. Nicole soon realized that her serve did not afford her the advantage she hoped for. Gail's returns were solid and reliable. Soon Gail had a 3-0 lead and was up 15-30 in game four. If the match continued the same way, a negative outcome was predictable. Nicole knew it. She needed to mix things up, and alter her game.

Drawing on inner strength, Nicole served with authority and recorded her first ace, tying the score at 30-30. Nicole changed the pace, and hit some higher balls with topspin from the baseline. She also hit short balls with under-spin and even drop shots to lure Gail to the net, where Nicole could lob over, pass, or confront Gail at the net. The change of pace paid off for Nicole. Gail, who regularly stayed a foot behind the baseline, was forced to resort to her net game; minimizing the utilization of her strong baseline game. Nicole won ten of the next twelve points to tie the score at 3-3.

It became a battle of wills. Nicole worked to shorten the points with an array of tennis skills. Gail did everything in her power to re-establish her ever-strong baseline game. The games went back and forth, with Gail's "Yes!" after each put-away point. However, Gail's success from the baseline was less apparent as Nicole became the aggressor. While she made a few errors on approach shots, generally the strategy paid off. Points were now much shorter. Nicole was more in control. Her ability to take advantage of her opponent at the net was starting to show. Winning five of six games, Nicole went up 5-4.

Nicole pushed extra hard to win the next game and took the set. After her serve was returned crisply to her forehand, she delivered a shot across court and retreated to the middle, at the baseline. The ball came back as if in a game of ping-pong. Nicole undercut a backhand shot across the court. Gail ran over, lifting the ball over the net, but the ball sat up. Nicole scampered in, and set herself. With Gail positioned at the net staring at her, Nicole walloped a winner that zoomed past Gail's shoulder, missing her by inches.

"Sorry, Gail. You okay?"

Gail was fuming. "Yeah," she shouted back. "No thanks to you!"

They split the next four points, each with a winner and an unforced error. The score was 40-30. Nicole lined up. She decided to serve and volley. She hit a solid first serve, and followed the ball to the net. By chance, Gail returned the ball with under-spin, leaving it short and Nicole was there ready to field it. Nicole lowered her racquet and flipped the ball just over the net for a perfect drop shot. Gail sprinted in, but the ball was unreachable.

Nicole felt fortunate to take the set. She realized that 6-4 was a narrow margin. The score could easily have been reversed. Visibly upset, Gail lined up to serve. She stood some five feet from her serving spot, her back to Nicole, and tried to gather herself. Suddenly she turned, rapidly approaching the line, and served. Although her attempt was well placed, Nicole returned it with ease, and once again the two were in the throes of a baseline tussle. Nicole kept the ball deep, but each shot was returned as hard as she sent it. The second set was much like the first, with each player trying to impose her will on the other. Gail continued her "Yes!" chant after each of her points.

In time Nicole's high, deep top-spin took its toll on Gail and resulted in short returns. Nicole took advantage of Gail's short balls; using approach shots to shorten the points. While Gail hit a few great passing shots, Nicole understood and expected no less from this seeded player. The set went to 5-5, with each player breaking the other's serve once. At 30-40, Gail served. The first serve went long. The second struck decisively—and Nicole stepped up and smacked it down the line for a winner.

Nicole found herself up; 6-5. She understood the importance of this game and knew that Gail was extremely dangerous. This game could prompt a momentum shift; Nicole definitely did not want to go to three sets.

A series of lengthy points took the game to 40-40; Nicole smoked a serve for an ace. It was match point. As the crowd grew quiet, Nicole took her time tossing the ball and serving it.

The serve clipped the top of the net and kicked out of bounds. The second serve came quickly. Gail made a solid return, and both girls fought from the baseline. After a dozen shots, Gail attempted a winner down the line. The ball hit the top of the net, skipped high, and landed just out, ending the set and giving Nicole the match; 6-4, 7-5.

For a split second, Nicole was tempted to cry out "Yes!" but quickly erased the thought from her mind. When the two met to shake hands, Nicole added, "Great match, Gail." Gail simply nodded, and remained silent all the way to the desk.

As Nicole met her family, Carol told her that Terry also won and would play again at 4:00. She left in a hurry after her match for some string repairs. They all chimed in, voicing their amazement at the high caliber of Nicole's match.

"The all-around game definitely made the difference," said Mia.

"I overheard several coaches talking about you after the match. They were very impressed with your game, but they all admitted they knew so little about your background. I found it amusing." Carol shared with Nicole.

As they approached the draw, a girl walked up to Nicole.

"You just beat Evans?" she asked incredulously.

Nicole nodded, and the girl continued, "Wow! I can't

believe you beat the "Little Rat!" as she walked off, shaking her head.

Nicole was now slotted in Gail's place, as if she were the sixth seed. Her next opponent, Tayler Shommer from Buffalo, New York, the eleventh seed, had already won and was off the court. The match would begin at 3:00. The tournament was down to sixteen in the main draw. Seeds were starting to play seeds. For another two rounds the back draw would continue to add players who had lost in the main draw.

"For a seventeenth-place finisher at the Westerns you are faring quite well, young lady."

Nicole smiled. "Thanks, Mia!"

Nicole had grown since Michigan. She had just won the biggest match of her life. Back at the hotel Nicole showered and changed. It was almost noon. Nicole was starving. For a change of pace, Jon chose the Putting Green Restaurant. The air-conditioning felt good as they sipped their iced tea. As they placed their orders, they could see Jon putting a few balls just outside the window. At once, he pointed to his putter, trying to send a message. Carol looked at Gram. "What is he saying?"

Mia smiled. "He's asking us to order the 'club' sandwich."

They laughed.

After lunch, Nicole went up to the room to rest for an hour. Shortly after 2:00, the Harris family returned to the Tennis Center. Again, the draw was their first stop. Except for Gail Evans, defeated by Nicole, all the seeds had held.

Mia quickly noted, "Only *three* members of the Wrecking Crew are left."

They grinned.

Nicole bumped into Amanda Cotton from Denver, still in the back draw and slated to play at 3:00 as well. They decided to warm up together. After about twenty minutes both girls felt ready. At the main desk, they joined their families to await their call. Soon Amanda was called, and shortly thereafter, Nicole heard her name called—"Harris, Shommer."

The eleventh seed from Buffalo, Tayler Shommer was about the same size as Nicole and was wearing a Niagara Falls t-shirt. On the way out, she asked Nicole what she thought about the banquet on the first night.

"I enjoyed it!" Nicole said.

"Did you have a good time?"

Tayler replied, "My parents liked the comedian, but I didn't think he was very funny!"

"Well, he was a little different," Nicole added.

"Thankfully, he wasn't here last year!"

As they began to warm up, Nicole noticed that Andrea Phillips, the number one seed, had arrived on the next court, set to play the sixteenth seed, Eve Kastenholz. After Nicole and Tayler finished a spirited warm-up, each was ready to go. The Harris family found a shady spot under an overhang to view the match. Nicole knew Mia was thankful. The girls spun the racquet, and Nicole won. They took their spots on the court.

Nicole's first serve missed. She readied herself, re-gripped her racquet, and set her feet. This time the serve was good, and Tayler returned the ball deep. Both girls hit the ball six times before Nicole drove the ball deep into the corner—a winner.

Since arriving, Nicole's confidence had skyrocketed. Aspects of her game— second serves, short balls, strategies— that had nagged her for so long, seemed distant memories. Nicole was playing with instinct, as if on auto-pilot. How fortunate she had been to have the help of Erin's family and coaches! To think it all started one fall day on the school court a short distance from home, when Dad introduced her to this game, she had come to love. She still played on that same court. He told her she had a special tennis talent. After his death, Nicole never thought she would ever feel up to playing tennis again. Time heals. The five long years had healed her intense grief and now Nicole found herself playing with far more purpose, as a tribute to the gift he had given her—a sheer love for the game.

Nicole re-focused, and served. Tayler returned the ball, this time a crisp shot to Nicole's backhand. From nearly a sitting position, Nicole blasted the ball back across the court for another winner; 30-0. On the next point Tayler hit her own winner down the line. Nicole's next serve hit the line, and scooted past her opponent. When the next point—after a series of shots—found the two girls face to face at the net, Tayler's volley did not have much on it. Nicole not only got to it, but put it firmly away to take the first game.

Not to be outdone, Tayler took game two with three powerful winners. Games one and two had taken twenty-five minutes. The girls seemed to be very evenly matched. Their size, their strokes, their play—at times mirrored each other almost eerily. Now, *no* points came easily. After an hour and ten minutes, the score was tied at 5-5.

Nicole lined up, served, hustled to return a short ball and hit it cleanly away for the point. The two split the next four points, as Tayler grew more aggressive. Up 40-30, Nicole served. Tayler sent the ball high and short over the net. Nicole rushed in, took the ball on the fly, and smashed a winner; 6-5.

The girls switched sides. If Nicole could break her, she could take the all-important first set. Tayler began with an ace, and followed with a winner down the line. Nicole responded with a forehand winner of her own. Tayler made a rare double-fault and followed with a backhand just wide. It was 30-40, set point. With the next point, the set would be Nicole's.

As Tayler got ready, Nicole jumped on two feet for rhythm, timed to react. The ball came, she pivoted and took it on the rise—and sent a bullet at Tayler's backhand. As the ball went over the net, it caught the tape, flipped in the air, and landed short, and out of reach on Tayler's side. Nicole took the first set.

Nicole was renewed with energy as she prepared to serve. This was definitely her best match, with very few errors. Her first-serve percentage was about 80%, but it had taken a momentous effort to just get by the first set. Tayler had a great game. She could be counted on to put up a good fight. Nicole knew Tayler would not give up and she needed to step up her game.

The second set was much like the first. Each girl held serve in a very close match. At 6-6, they went to a tiebreaker. Just as the match had been close, so was the tiebreaker. Each held serve. The score was 4-4. The winner needed seven points and a margin of two points. As Nicole lined up, a scream erupted two courts away. Nicole paused, and she and Tayler both instinctively turned their heads towards the commotion. A voice was heard—"Man, come on! Open your eyes!" Mr. Badad from Chicago was reacting to his daughter's scream. His daughter, Brenda, the eighth seed, was playing a girl from Tallahassee.

Several officials ran over, talked to the girls and Mr. Badad, and remained on the court. They decided to officiate the remainder of the match.

"Are you ready?" Nicole called, and Tayler nodded. Nicole served—her first ace of the tiebreaker. Up 5-4, she had to break Tayler. Tayler's first serve careened out. Nicole stepped up and took the second serve on the rise, sending it to the corner. As Tayler hit a running backhand, Nicole moved in, correctly guessing the placement of the return, and hit a forehand volley to the opposite court for a winner.

It was double set, match point. As Tayler tossed the ball, Nicole gripped her racquet solidly, and quickly pivoted for a forehand. Again she caught the ball on the rise, sending it down the line with no chance of a return. She took the set and the match; 7-5, 7-6.

At the net the girls shook hands. It had been a long match, two and a half hours. As they wished each other luck and headed in to report the score. Nicole was in a near-daze. She couldn't believe she was in the final eight.

The family was waiting to congratulate her and check the draw. The Badads were at the draw, too. Brenda won and would face Andrea. At 9:00 tomorrow, Nicole would meet the number three seed, Jessica Rimmer from Kansas City, Missouri, who just won 6-3, 6-3 over the fourteen seed, Sally Cavanaugh from Provo, Utah. Sadly, Terry just lost 6-4, 6-4, to Amy Hauser. With her second loss, her play was over. The Smiths won their first three doubles matches. Nicole looked for Terry, unsuccessfully.

They headed back to the hotel. Although Nicole was tired, Mia announced a special treat. "I'm going to treat everyone to Red Lobster for dinner," adding, "We all need a change of pace."

It was after 6:30 when they arrived and were seated in their booth. The restaurant was very busy. They were glad they arrived when they did and were happy to be seated so quickly. They had been to Red Lobster only once, for Mia's birthday. Everyone loved it. When the waitress came to the table, they all ordered the fried shrimp. Mia smiled and asked Nicole, "Is *that* on your special diet?"

The dinner was delicious. Just before they finished, Mr. Nelson, who had been sitting with another gentleman near-by, walked over. "Nicole—great job!" he exclaimed. He introduced the other gentleman, Jim Ellison, a local pro. "Nicole, you are really playing well. I'm impressed," Jim said. Since most of the girls have departed for home by now, he offered to warm Nicole up.

"Wow, I would really appreciate that," she replied.

They agreed to meet at 8:15. "I have some information we can go over as well," he added.

"Thanks a million," Nicole replied.

"Well, get a good night's sleep," he said. "I'll see you in the morning."

Suddenly there was an outburst by the cash register—a loud, familiar voice—"That's it! *No* tip!!"

Mr. Badad exited angrily.

After dinner, the Harrises returned to the hotel. Carol and Mia were excited. A new show, *Seinfeld*, debuted last week. They loved the show because it was different, and were curious to see if the second show would be as funny as the first. "That Kramer character was a real stitch," Mia remarked.

After the show, Nicole set her alarm, requested a wake-up call, and fell fast asleep.

# STRIVE FOR A CONSISTENT,
# ALL-AROUND GAME

Mia called in to Nicole and Jon just before the alarm went off. Nicole got up, and pulled open the drapes, to an overcast, dreary sky. Nicole went through her routine, and everyone met down at breakfast by 7:30. Mia asked Nicole if her headbands were okay. Nicole looked at her oddly, and shook her head. "We just don't want any uniform malfunctions," Mia smirked.

Nicole didn't eat much, and seemed nervous. Carol insisted she eat at least some oatmeal, and drink some juice. Nicole went up to the room to stretch. After, Mia gathered the family for a short prayer, and they were off.

At the Tennis Center, a sizable crowd was present. On one side several college coaches were having an animated discussion. Nicole checked in and spotted Jim. The two went to a nearby court to warm up. As they started, a slight breeze came up, chilling the air ever so slightly. Jim had great strokes. The ball came off his racquet smoothly, effortlessly. Jim did not offer a single piece of advice during the warm-up. Instead, he continually reinforced—"Great shot! Great shot!"

When Nicole indicated she was ready, he walked over and told her he had seen Jessica Rimmer play. He shared a few observations, and offered a few suggestions on aspects of Jessica's game that Nicole might try to exploit.

"Nicole, just be yourself and play your game," he concluded.

"Play with heart and courage. The rest will take care of itself."

At these words Nicole smiled, and visibly relaxed. In so many words Jim had confirmed that her game was sufficient.

"Thank you, so much Jim. Your kind words mean a lot. I appreciate you warming me up, too."

At the tournament desk he told her, "I'd wish you good luck, Nicole, but you don't need it. You have something better—skill and determination. Now go out and show it on the court!"

With this, he vanished into the crowd, leaving her to rejoin her family.

In the main draw only eight girls remained but in the back draw several matches were yet to be played. The crowd buzzed about the upcoming "Match of the Day." By far, the match-up that generated the most interest was the one between the number one seed Andrea and Brenda Badad, the eighth seed.

"There'll be some fireworks in that match!" someone was overheard commenting.

"Rimmer, Harris" echoed the tournament director. The match was held on one of the smaller stadium courts.

Jessica and Nicole shook hands and moved to the court. Jessica was a 5'10" blond. Her T-shirt—"Arch Deluxe"—showed the picture of an arch like the famous St. Louis Gateway. Nicole wondered if it was an indication of her love for lobs. As for Nicole, she wore one of the outfits Mia made and gave her last Christmas.

As the two warmed up, a small crowd assembled. With

the sun not a factor, Mia, Carol, and Jon sat comfortably in the stands. The girls met at the net. Jessica spun her racquet. Nicole won and elected to serve first. After a quick drink, they assumed their spots on the baseline. The winner would advance to the final four.

Nicole took a deep breath, and made the toss. Her serve was returned sharply. At once the two were in a furious baseline rally, each girl refusing to yield an inch. Each hit the ball at least fourteen times before Jessica's shot caught the net, lifted high into the air, and fell short on Nicole's side. Nicole rushed in, and put the ball away for a winner. Nicole smashed her next serve with power and authority, producing a short return. Again she rushed in and put the ball away, this time to the other corner. On the next point, Nicole hit a forehand wide after retreating to the baseline to return a colossal forehand of Jessica's. Though early in the match, play was already heating up. With another solid serve, Nicole aced Jessica to the inside, and was now up 40-15. The next point found the girls fighting another lengthy rally. Nicole finally broke through by smashing a forehand to Jessica's backhand deep on the court. Ever vigilant, Nicole took advantage of the short return with a winner, short and angled off the court, taking the first game.

Quickly Jessica won game two much like Nicole had won game one. Nicole hit a few short balls and paid the price. Additionally, Jessica recorded her first ace. Then both girls held serve and the match was tied up at 2-2. As Nicole stepped up to serve game five, Jessica hit under-spin approach shots to get herself to the net. She had also served and volleyed on the last point. Nicole thought back to the warm-up, and remembered Jim's advice, to avoid Jessica's lethal forehand, and to closely watch Jessica's under-spin approach shots, since they oftentimes sat up, ripe for the picking. Jim urged Nicole to pay close attention, to recognize and take advantage of that shot—turning it into her own approach shot. Finally, he advised Nicole to hit whenever possible to Jessica's backhand, since it was far more probable to produce a short ball.

All this advice made good sense, and Nicole was determined to use it. As she prepared, a few raindrops fell on her arm and the back of her neck. Despite the weather, she opened the game with an ace—and won seven of the next nine points, for a 4-2 lead. Hitting to Jessica's backhand made a huge difference, and enabled Nicole to sneak to the net. Jessica, undaunted, pushed even harder. At 5-4, Jessica started to serve game ten. Nicole pounded the return solidly and got to the net, resulting in a crisp volley for a winner. Then Nicole won the next two points by out-dueling Jessica from the baseline. On the last point of game ten, Nicole hit a crushing forehand to Jessica's backhand. When she followed it in, expecting a short passing shot, she encountered a lob, but was able to hit a powerful overhead to the opposite side and take the set, 6-4.

Nicole was relieved. Although the heavier rain held off, the drops continued to fall. Jessica started the new set strongly, advancing to a 3-2 lead. Recognizing Nicole's backhand tactic, she began running around her backhand to use her strong forehand. Her serve, too, was starting to click.

The next two games exhibited how closely the girls were matched skill-wise. Each played her heart out. Each game went to deuce several times. Game seven of this set included nine deuce points. Lengthy rallies marked each point. Neither player would give in. But somehow, some way, Nicole found opportunities, and won both games. By the time Jessica served at 3-4, the momentum had shifted. Losing the last two games had been devastating for Jessica. She was very distracted and recorded two uncharacteristic double-faults in the next game.

Nicole quickly won the next two points, then served for the match. Feeling very confident and in control, Nicole hit three aces, and took the match 6-4, 6-3.

Nicole answered the call and played the best tennis of her life. As the two made their way to the desk, Mr. Nelson and Jim offered congratulations. "I have *never* seen you play like you did today!" Mr. Nelson beamed. "Way to go, Nicole," Jim added. "You really played your game and took advantage of opportunities. If you'd like, I can meet you at 2:15 to warm you up for your next match."

Nicole agreed. After she and Jessica reported the score, she joined her family. Grinning ear to ear, Mia shook her head. "Simply amazing," she said.

"I'll second that," added Carol.

"Wow! Way to *go*, Sis!" exclaimed Jon.

Now in the final four, Nicole would play again at 3:00. Her opponent, number-two seed Shannon Meyers from Las Vegas had earned an impressive 6-2, 6-3 victory over the tenacious Barb Luebstorf from Louisville. Meanwhile, there had been no more screams in the Phillips–Badad match. Andrea won easily, 6-2, 6-0. She would face the Western District's top player, Sara Luvell from Indianapolis, in the other semi-final. With rain threatening, the director declared it was imperative to finish the semis. Tomorrow's final match was scheduled to be televised.

As the Harrises departed, several call out "Great job, Nicole!" and "Good luck at three!" Nicole smiled and thanked them. She could finish no less than fourth in the whole country! She had exceeded her own expectations by far, but didn't want it to end there. She was a different player now. She had tasted victory on the big stage, and wanted more.

After Nicole's quick shower, the Harrises went to the Golf restaurant—Jon's choice. During lunch, several came in from the golf green. It started drizzling steadily. Would the matches go on? Nicole wondered. Regardless, she intended to meet Jim at 2:15 and be ready to compete. She started to mentally prepare, no matter what the circumstance.

As the Harrises made their way back, dark ominous clouds gathered, wind speeds picked up, and heavy rain was threatening. Mr. Nelson was waiting with Jim, ready to warm up on Court Two. Already Andrea and several pros were hitting on the stadium court. Shannon was on another court and on the farthest court was Sara, Andrea's next opponent. Jim once again succeeded in relaxing Nicole with the warm-up. As they practiced, sporadic drops came down. Nicole had played in the rain with Mr. Novak and had drilled solo on rainy days against the board at the park, but had never played in a match setting.

Within fifteen minutes all four girls stood at the tournament desk, ready to start. A sizeable crowd had convened, including many of the coaches. After a few minutes, the officials summoned the girls to the desk. The director announced that the matches *would* be played today. All four looked at each other and smiled in anticipation. Andrea and Sara would play on the main stadium court; Nicole and Shannon on the smaller stadium court adjacent.

After another ten-minute warm-up, Nicole and Shannon met at the net. Shannon won the racquet spin and chose to serve. With raindrops falling, Nicole wore a visor along with her headband. The girls lined up on their baselines, and the semi-finals began.

Shannon started the match demonstrating her powerful serve. Late with her response, Nicole returned it wide. She moved over, a bit dejected, and returned the next serve short and up the middle. Shannon deftly ran around the ball and delivered an inside-out forehand to Nicole's backhand side—a winner.

"Come on, Nicole—you need to concentrate right now!" Nicole mentally challenged herself.

Her heart racing, she sighed and prepared for the next

point. The serve came, long. As the next attempt came, Nicole stepped forward and took the ball on the rise, driving it into the corner for a winner. Shannon's next serve hit the inside line—a winner.

Up 40-15, Shannon missed her next attempt, but placed her second serve in, and for the first time, the two rallied from the baseline. Before long, Shannon smoked the ball into the corner to Nicole's backhand. Nicole ran over, as Shannon edged up to the net. Not able to get enough of the ball to pass her, Nicole decided on a lob, which ended up short. Shannon retreated back, caught the ball perfectly, and hit an overhead winner to the opposite corner. Game One went to Shannon.

The girls switched sides and got a quick drink. It was up to Nicole to take control and hold serve. Her first offering was long. She sighed, readied herself, and served. Again the two rallied. After Nicole hit a short ball, Shannon jumped all over it with a topspin approach shot to Nicole's forehand. As she followed the ball in, Nicole was only able to deliver a weak return that Shannon volleyed for a clear winner. Then Shannon attacked Nicole's first serve. Guessing right, she delivered a winner. Frustrated, Nicole double-faulted, making the score love–40. Nicole's next serve was a winner, but Shannon responded to Nicole's next serve with a winner of her own, increasing the game totals to 2-0.

Shannon was quick to serve and kept the action going. Winning four out of five points with the help of two aces, she easily took game three. As the rain continued, Nicole lined up. It had been a long time since she had lost three straight games. Amid her frustration, she could hear the cheers prompted by points from the other match. She resumed play, and finally won game four after going to deuce three times. Once again Shannon came back strong, winning the next three games to take the set, 6-1.

The rain persisted as Nicole lined up. Would it ever stop? Nicole knew that Shannon faced the same weather conditions. Shannon however, appeared to be doing a better job of ignoring it. With the first game of the second set so important, Nicole had to make a statement. Shannon understood, too, and both girls became very aggressive. At 40-40 Nicole hit a second serve. Shannon belted it back. The ball hit the net and dropped over on Nicole's side; ad-out. The rain started to pick up, along with the wind as Nicole served, prompting a lengthy rally, until Nicole's forehand drifted wide.

Suddenly, officials stopped both matches and instructed the girls to retire to a locker room under the bleachers to sit out the weather privately with their families. Nicole was down 6-1, 1-0, and had lost the last four games. Andrea won the first set over Sara, 6-3, and was up, 4-1, in the second.

Nicole was visibly sad. Carol smiled and tried to cheer her up. Jon gave her a hug.

"Don't worry, Nicole," said Gram. "You'll be O.K."

Nicole could only shake her head and confessed, "I'm thinking too much out there. I just need to relax."

It took a solid hour for the rain to let up. The

officials asked for volunteers to join the Squeegee Crew to help ready the courts. Carol volunteered, and Jon went to watch. Everyone was hopeful that play would resume within fifteen minutes.

Alone with Nicole, Mia turned serious. "Nicole," she started, "Listen to me. My parents took a mighty big chance coming over to this country a long time ago. They bucked the odds, but they made it. I always wished I could have continued with tennis, but seeing you play makes me so happy. I hate to see you so miserable now. You were put into this position. Things happen for a reason. I feel it. Your Mom and Jon love you. I love you. Erin and her family love you and care about you deeply. Your Dad loved you very much and gave you a great start. I know he's sharing these moments right here with you now. Nicole, there's always an answer if you look deep into your heart. We love you. We want you to win. But what we really want is for you to *try* and *do your best*. Remember, *Love must mean something!*"

A loud-speaker beckoned the players. Nicole hugged Mia warmly, gathered her gear, and left to resume the match. The Squeegee Crew had done an amazing job. The courts were virtually dry. Only a few wet spots remained on the edges of each court. While it was only 5:20 p.m., the lights were turned on, since it had grown quite dark. As she took her spot for the five-minute warm-up, Nicole was wearing her NH headband and was now using her wooden Chris Everett racquet. As she went through the paces in her spirited warm-up, an old, familiar, determined look came to her face.

Play resumed. Shannon's first serve was long. Her second struck directly in the service box. Nicole gauged, took the ball on the rise, and sent it to the right corner—a winner. Shannon's next serve prompted a rally, until Nicole dropped an unexpected short shot just over the net—another winner. Nicole was determined. She would dictate the match on *her* terms. Flustered, Shannon responded with a double-fault; love–40.

Now Shannon took her time and she delivered a booming serve. Nicole turned her hips and blocked the ball with a short forehand stroke. The ball hit the racquet with an odd sound and sent the ball lamely toward the top of the net. The ball hit the tape, and fell on Shannon's side. Nicole broke Shannon's serve and won the game incredibly in four straight points.

Nicole studied her prized racquet her dad had given her. She noticed the deep crack in the frame between the handle and the strings. Sadly, she walked over to fetch Erin's racquet, kissing the old racquet before gently sliding it into the case.

"I'm sorry, Dad," she whispered.

She had not used the racquet since the Westerns, but it still wielded its magic, producing four of the biggest points of her life. *Had* she received help from above?

Nicole grabbed the racquet with a prominent E.N. on its handle, and ambled back to her spot like a prizefighter responding to the bell. She would serve. She had a chance to take the lead in the set. A warm confidence flooded through her as she lined up.   Her serve generated a short return, which she drove into the corner. Shannon responded with a backhand passing shot, but Nicole cut the ball off with a volley to the opposite court—a winner. Nicole's next two serves were aces, landing just inside the service box; 40-love. After a series of topspin forehands pinned Shannon deep on the baseline, a drop shot won the game.

The players split the next six games, each game extremely close. Now Shannon once again surged. As Nicole readied to receive, a score went up; Andrea had just beat Sara, 6-3, 6-3. Determined to break Shannon's serve and claim the second set, Nicole smacked her first two service returns for winners, then hit the third into the net. She bounced around freely now, like Ali in his famous rope-a-dope. Nicole blocked the next offering, sending it deep in the corner. Off the short return she hit a backhand under-spin up the line. Shannon ran over, and tried to lift the ball over Nicole. Positioned at the service line, Nicole gauged, took a step back, and delivered a powerful overhead—a winner.

Now double set point, Nicole blocked Shannon's serve with a shot deep to her backhand. Shannon ran the ball down, and delivered the ball up the line. Nicole raced toward the sideline in anticipation, noting that Shannon had a very small a window of opportunity. Shannon's shot landed wide. Set two went to Nicole, 6-4.

As the girls changed sides, Nicole peeked up at her family. They were 'all smiles.' Mia nodded. Carol blew a kiss. With Mia's handmade towel, Nicole dried her face and her arms, before returning to the court to start the third set.

She was energized now, ready to play her game. Since the delay, she was concentrating much better and was reacting to the challenge with renewed zeal.

Nicole gripped Erin's racquet, making her toss. Her serve was blocked back. With small stutter steps, Nicole made her way to the ball, addressed it, and returned it hard to Shannon's backhand, deep in the court. Shannon could only block the shot, returning it short, near the service line. Nicole scampered in, and hit it at its apex away from her opponent, for a winner. Nicole crushed a serve directly at Shannon, handcuffing her, and the ball skidded off her racquet and landed near the bench area; 30-love.

Nicole felt much better, far more in control. The next three points were played from each baseline, with the last shot a backhand up the line that landed directly on the line itself. Nicole won two of the points and the first game. Even though Shannon had more games—ten to seven—Nicole was ahead, up in the third set. If she broke her opponent only once and held serve, she would win the match.

"This is the game!" she told herself.

Nicole swayed back and forth and then took a two-foot hop as Shannon made contact with the ball. This found her in perfect balance to field the serve equally well in either direction.

Nicole returned the first offering with a deep cross-court forehand. Somewhat off balance, Shannon managed to hit the ball back safely. The two traded strokes, until Shannon hit a short return. Nicole ran up and placed a drop shot just over the net. Frustrated, Shannon screamed loudly. She had no chance to retrieve the shot. With this, her first public display of frustration, Nicole knew that Shannon would come on strong. The next serve went long, and Nicole edged up a couple of feet and readied herself. Next came a spin serve. Nicole took it on the rise and sent it like a rope deep to Shannon's forehand side—a winner.

Shannon slowly fetched the ball and returned to the service area. She took a deep breath, and tossed the ball. Her serve was in, and a rally ensued. After a dozen shots, Shannon's backhand went long; love-40.

The pressure was almost tangible. If Nicole won one of the next three points, she would have the service break she so desperately needed. Shannon hit a booming serve and followed it in, expecting a weak return. Nicole barely got a racquet on the ball, sending it meagerly just over the net. Waiting patiently, Shannon slammed the ball away; 15–40.

Nicole returned the next serve deep to the middle of the court. Shannon responded with a shot to Nicole's forehand. Nicole lined up, pointed her left foot, and sent a crushing forehand down the line that Shannon was unable to reach; 2-0.

Nicole held serve for her next three games, as did Shannon. Now 5-3, Nicole was serving for the match. The last six games had been close. Shannon was a tenacious opponent, unwilling to yield an inch. Lining up for her first attempt, Nicole viewed Shannon moving in and out, back and forth, like a caged animal ready to spring.

"Finish! Nicole mentally challenged herself as she tossed the ball into the air.

The serve was returned solidly, and both girls moved to the ball like there was no tomorrow—there wasn't. Nicole hit the ball back to the middle of the court. Shannon ran around it, preparing a big forehand, and smoked the ball in the corner to Nicole's backhand side. Nicole sprinted over to retrieve it as Shannon raced to the net. Desperate, Nicole hit a backhand topspin lob to the opposite corner, just over Shannon's outstretched racquet. The ball landed in the corner as Shannon ran after it, with no chance of a return. Turning a negative into a positive, Nicole felt some relief.

Shannon slammed Nicole's next serve back for a winner. As the ball landed, Shannon yelled "Yes!" and pumped her fist; 15-15. The two split the next four points on a series of baseline exchanges resulting in another tie score; 40-40. Nicole's served a 'boomer' that landed very close to Shannon, leaving her no room to swing. She did, however, get a racquet on the ball, which sailed off the court; match point.

Nicole served—long. As she prepared for her second serve, Shannon edged closer and returned the ball to Nicole's forehand. Nicole scampered over to hit the ball—a running forehand down the line. Anticipating, Shannon moved over to volley the ball. Shannon's shot was in, but not very deep, leaving Nicole time to run the ball down with Shannon waiting at the net. As Nicole ran left, Shannon mirrored her. Now in position to make a play, Nicole couldn't get enough on the ball to pass or lob, so she decided to ease the ball sideways across court and again moved Shannon. As she hit the ball, her momentum carried Nicole off the court. As she stopped, she turned her head and peeked back. The ball caught the top of the net on the far side and fell softly on Shannon's side. Shannon sprinted over and tried to scoop the ball, but to no avail.

Nicole survived. Her come-from-behind 1-6, 6-4, 6-3 victory had earned her a place in the championship. The eighty-plus fans who just witnessed the match gave the girls a standing ovation as they shook hands. It had been a long, draining day. The match began at 3:00; and ended at 7:45. As the girls reported the score, Mrs. Sullivan told them to report at 11:00 tomorrow. The final match would start at noon. Shannon and Sara would play for third place.

The family congratulated Nicole with hugs.

"I just knew you would find a way, little girl. I just *knew*!" said Mia.

"We all did," said Carol.

"Slap me five— you're still alive!!" grinned Jon.

Nicole was smiling but tired and very sore as they returned to the car. In the lot beside them a TV truck was parked. They planned to eat quickly before returning to the hotel for showers. They chose Perkins, and ate in forty minutes. They arrived back at the hotel after 9:00. Nicole took a long, hot shower and rested her feet. They sat in the living room and talked. Tomorrow was Sunday, the last day. They found a 10:00 service at Immaculata Catholic Church, right on campus. This would work perfectly. Already 10 p.m., one by one, they said their goodnights and headed to their beds for a good night sleep.

# ASSESS YOUR OPPONENT

At 8 a.m. Carol walked in announcing, "Good morning, sleepy heads. I have some bad news. It's raining cats and dogs out there. This *is* going to be an issue today."

Nicole and Jon jumped up and peeked out the window. The rain was descending in thick curtains.

"We'll just have to see what the officials decide," said Carol.

They dressed, and Nicole did her stretching. As they ate breakfast at the Pool Restaurant, the rain continued. Stiff gusts of wind erupted. It even looked like there were whitecaps on the pool.

"Boy, for this match to happen, the Squeegee Crew *will* have to perform magic," said Mia.

"That's my department!" responded Carol.

They arrived at Immaculata Catholic church, a large, beautiful, ornate structure of stained glass and unique architecture. Carol said it reminded her of churches she had seen in photos of Italy. In an alcove Nicole lit candles for her two angels—Dad and Erin. She apologized to Dad about the racquet and hoped he would be there today to support her. She thanked Erin for being such a great friend, and thanked them both for helping her. Their love was carrying her through the tournament. Finally, she asked God to help her to play her best—no more, no less.

Father Andrew's homily offered a great, relevant message of love. He reminded the packed church. "God is love. He sent his Son to teach us to love one another without expecting anything in return."

The family was comforted and inspired by the message.

Once at the Tennis Center, some thirty people were huddled under the pavilion. Mrs. Sullivan, the director, announced, "The forecast is for rain, all day. So we will move the matches to 11:00 a.m. tomorrow. Fox Channel Six still hopes to cover the event."

Mr. Nelson and Jim told Nicole to be ready to warm up at 10 tomorrow, and everyone left.

Back at the hotel, Nicole was antsy. She couldn't go through a day without a workout and tennis. She had the perfect remedy. Unable to play indoors during the winter, she developed an indoor routine she performed in her basement. Now was as good a time as any to use her old routine to keep herself active. For the next hour and a half she did sit-ups, pushups, stretches, burpees, jumping jacks, foot-fires. She ran in place, practiced her strokes by simulating contact and follow-through. After her workout, she felt energized and content. With no indoor courts available, she once again was able to turn a negative into a positive.

Meanwhile, Carol worked feverishly to make flight changes. She left a message at St. Elizabeth's notifying the office that both children would miss the first day of school. In the afternoon, with rain still descending, they decided to see a movie at a local theater—Jon's choice, *Hoosiers*. The film, with Gene Hackman and Barbara Hershey, they all enjoyed. Carol mentioned that Dad would have really appreciated it.

"I'm going to be a basketball player, just like Dad," said Jon.

That night they dined at the Golf restaurant and turned in early. The weather channel predicted the front would leave, and promised better weather.

They awoke to a beautiful Monday—the sun shining, 78 degrees. What a difference!

"If you could be granted one wish, what would it be?" Carol asked Nicole.

"Excluding the 'candy tree,' that I play my best and Dad and Erin could be here with us." Nicole answered without hesitation.

"This *is* going to be an awesome day," Carol emphatically stated.

After Nicole stretched, they ate breakfast. By 10 they were at the Tennis Center. Jim and Mr. Nelson were already there, waiting. A crowd started to gather. The Channel Six live truck was on site. Andrea was walking on the stadium court with several people who appeared to be pros. Sara and Shannon were warming up. The atmosphere was electric.

It would be Nicole's last match of the season. As she took out her racquet, she peered over to see Andrea confidently and methodically, hitting balls. Coaches occupied the stands with Mr. Nelson, along with other players, and a few hotel workers whom the Harrises had befriended. Cameras were set up at two spots on the court. An announcer presided. Soon, some five hundred were in attendance.

Jim and Nicole hit for half an hour. Jim made a few

suggestions and they finished with an emphasis on service return. Jim declared, "Young lady, you are *ready*!"

"Thanks a million, Jim."

Nicole spent a few moments with her family. When the call came, they all hugged her and wished her good luck. As she departed, Jon yelled to her— "Sis, just remember. This court is the same size as the one back home in Hickory!"

Nicole smiled, and made her way to the desk. There she met Andrea, who was two inches taller and at least fifteen pounds heavier. She appeared very fit, and ready to play with her blonde hair tied-back, a striking contrast to her brilliant tan. Nicole shook Andrea's hand.

"Good luck today," Nicole told her opponent.

"The same to you!" Andrea responded.

It had been less than a year ago that Nicole, the Milwaukee County Champ, had watched from her living room as Andrea dismantled her opponent on national television. Nicole felt confident and did not plan to become one more of Andrea's victims. She would be a full-fledged *opponent*. As the two stepped out onto the court and began to hit, Andrea stared intently, assessing Nicole's every move. Several ball boys made their way to the court. The chair umpire was already in place. Out of Nicole's earshot a TV announcer, Mr. Harper, labeled the match "David versus Goliath."

Nicole spun her racquet, the E.N. showing prominently. Andrea won the spin and would serve first.

"Ladies and gentlemen, this does not appear to be a good

omen for Ms. Harris," confided the announcer. "It must be like looking down the barrel of a lethal weapon to start this match!"

The girls took their spots. Nicole was overcome with goose bumps, and her palms were sweaty. Mia had assured her that once the match began, it would be just like any other. At this point, however, it didn't seem very logical. Nicole knew of Andrea's reputation for big serves. They could intimidate and devastate an opponent in a relatively short period of time. She would have to be on her toes from the start.

As Andrea began her service motion, Nicole moved back and forth, and on Andrea's racquet contact, came to a jump stop. The ball whizzed past—just long. Nicole took a deep breath as she lined up for the second serve. The serve was good and Nicole let loose, took the ball on the rise and smacked it like a bullet down the line, with no chance of return. The crowd buzzed; love–15. Nicole was up!

Andrea lined up, and her serve hit the mark. Nicole once again was able to return the ball, this time deep in the middle. Andrea returned to Nicole's backhand and made her way up to the service area. Nicole scampered over, set herself, pointed her right foot, and delivered a crisp backhand down the line that just cleared the net and sunk just below Andrea's outstretched racquet.

"Wow!" commented the announcer. "Andrea has lost only one service game in the entire tournament and already Nicole is threatening in game one!"

Andrea's next serve was a booming ace to the middle of the court. "Nice shot!" Nicole called as they moved over; 15-30. Nicole returned the next serve, and the two rallied from the baseline. Eventually Nicole hit an inside-out forehand to Andrea's backhand and edged up to the service line. Andrea hit a running backhand short and crosscourt that appeared to sink quickly over the net. Nicole cross-stepped with her right foot and extended her racquet. The ball hit her racquet and softly made its way back over the net; 15-40.

"Ahhhh!" Andrea yelled in frustration. Again she delivered a big serve that handcuffed Nicole leaving her no shot; 30-40.

Nicole quickly realized that her chance of victory would be linked to her return of serve. Thankfully, this had always been one of the strongest aspects of her game. Nicole, confident, returned the next offering right back at Andrea, who sent an off-balance shot deep, back to Nicole. The girls were now toe to toe at the baseline. Each hit the ball four times as if probing for a weakness. Finally, Andrea ran around a ball and hit a formidable forehand deep in the corner to Nicole's backhand. Nicole ran down the ball as Andrea hastily approached. On the run, Nicole sent a topspin lob cross-court just over Andrea's outstretched racquet. The ball nicked Andrea's racquet and landed deep in the corner, bouncing high against the wall, leaving Andrea watching.

Game one was Nicole's. The girls got water and changed sides. "Come on Andrea—let's *go!*" a voice sounded.

Mr. Harper was dumbfounded as he told the audience,

"Nicole has already tied the number of games Andrea has lost serving in the entire tournament and it is *only game one.*"

Nicole understood that if she could hold serve, a first-set victory was definitely possible. However, she needed to concentrate on each point, not look too far in advance. As she lined up, she glanced over at Andrea, who seemed a bit upset. Nicole's first serve came blasting back like a cannon shot—a winner deep to the backhand.

"Yesssss!" Andrea yelled, pumped her fist, and strutted back to her position.

"What a return!" said Harper. "This match *has* heated up in a hurry."

Nicole responded with a solid serve that Andrea barely returned over the net. Nicole ran up and tapped the ball back—a fine drop shot, good; 15-15.

The players split the next four points, each making an unforced error, to leave the score at deuce. Nicole's next serve drew a sharp return. With Andrea well behind the baseline, she hit an under-spin shot that totally surprised Andrea. The ball made its way just over the net and fell, irretrievable; ad-in.

Having success with so many shots gave Nicole a sense of control, increasing her confidence even more. The next serve—her own version of a cannon shot—struck just outside of the line. Andrea viewed the line judge almost in disgust, until she realized the 'out' call. Nicole resorted to her second serve, but the ball sat up. Andrea was ready, but in her haste she hit the ball cleanly but a shade long. Game - Nicole. The crowd oohed and aahed.

"Ladies and gentlemen, Andrea has never been down in this tournament," said Harper. "With a 2-0 score, Ms. Harris *is* making a definite statement."

The ball boy presented Andrea with two balls. She took her spot, looking very determined as she tossed. The ball came off her strings with a loud pop, hit the line and streaked right by Nicole—an ace. Again the crowd oohed. Next came a booming serve only inches from the last spot—another ace. The next serve Nicole managed to return, but weakly. Andrea ran up and delivered—a winner off the side of the court. Finally, another big serve that Nicole hit into the net.

Andrea came back with vengeance, and took every point in game three. She strutted over for a drink on the changeover.

"Now *that's* the Andrea we know from last year. *That's* what we've been talking about!" The announcer told the television audience.

Nicole paused to regain her composure, and headed over to serve. After all, it was only one game and serving was her strong suit, the score was still 2-1, she reminded herself. She took a deep breath, tossed the ball, ever-visualizing the ball clearing the net and exploding. The serve cleared, and was returned deep to her backhand. Nicole returned the ball across court to Andrea's backhand. If anything, this might be a weaker part of Andrea's game. Andrea returned the ball, but with nowhere near the power of her forehand. After several backhands, Nicole decided to run around the ball and go for the line. Her shot was crisp, and Andrea was unable to reach it.

Next, Nicole served and aced Andrea. Up 30-love, Nicole missed her next first serve but the second serve had a great kick that neutralized the return. Andrea did, however, get the ball deep again to Nicole's backhand. They rallied several times before Andrea let loose with a penetrating forehand. Nicole's running backhand returned up the line was promptly intercepted by Andrea's soft volley to the opposite court, for the point.

Nicole answered back—a big serve that Andrea hit into the net.

"Who would have figured Andrea would get a dose of her own arsenal?" asked Harper.

At 40-15, Nicole was serving for the game. Missing her first, she also erred on the second—her first double-fault. Andrea smiled as she moved over. Nicole's next offering came right back at her. With Andrea edging slightly to her right back to the middle, Nicole smoked an inside-out forehand cross court that stayed in and angled off the court near the service line.

The crowd cheered. It was a chancy shot, but Nicole pulled it off. It was now 1-3, with Andrea serving.

"This young lady from Milwaukee is for *real*, folks," Harper announced.

Each player held serve for the next four games, bringing the score to 5-3. Andrea served next.

"America, Andrea has not lost a set all year!" the announcer remarked.

Andrea was determined that this would not be the first time. Once again she held serve—three aces and a fine serve and volley, closing the game score to 5-4.

Could Nicole answer? This game would be huge. Winning it would give Nicole the set.

Nicole secured the balls from the ball boy, slipped one into her tennis pocket, and lined up. Her toss and serve were perfect, but Andrea sent a hard return right at Nicole's feet. Nicole got a racquet on the ball, lifting it high toward the rushing Andrea, who feasted on the lame duck with a crushing overhead.

The crowd gasped. A bit shaken herself, Nicole took a moment. Seconds later she was ready and returned to the line serving with a vengeance, forcing Andrea to return her serve wide; 15-15.

Andrea hit  Nicole's next serve long with a powerful forehand, but Nicole then hit  an easy forehand wide; 30-30. Nicole's next serve was good; its return took her back to the baseline for a backhand. Her stroke was perfect. Andrea turned her body, and smacked a backhand down the line. The ball caught the very top of the net and skipped out of bounds. Andrea unsuccessfully took a chance with not only her backhand, but her decision to send the ball where the net was at its highest point. It was now 40-30; set point Nicole.

Nicole lined up, took a deep breath, and tossed. Andrea responded with a backhand to mid-court. Nicole moved her feet into proper position. With Andrea moving towards the middle, Nicole hit a forehand in Andrea's direction, a little behind her. Andrea attempted to stop, to play the ball, but could only get the edge of her racquet on the ball.

Nicole won the first set, 6-4. The crowd cheered not only the winner, but the gutsy choice of shots.

"Way to go, Sis!" yelled Jon.

"Holy smokes!" said Harper. "This is the first set Andrea has lost in the tournament and I believe all year."

Back in Milwaukee, Dr. Stanwood smiled as he watched in the hospital father's lounge. Carol's colleagues came out ever so often to peek. Mr. Novak had taken the day off and was enjoying every minute. At St. Elizabeth, Nicole's class watched the match on a classroom TV under a sign, FOR EDUCATIONAL PURPOSES ONLY, and cheered loudly. Sister Clara smiled, and tried to quiet them.

Back on the court in San Diego, Nicole was elated, but knew that the fight had just begun. Andrea, visibly angry, stalked to the service area with a rigid, pale face.

"Get ready, folks. Nicole's victory in set one just may have started World War III!" announced Harper.

The crowd fell silent. Andrea uncoiled into her patented service motion, and exploded on the ball—an ace. The ball boy ran up. Andrea took the ball and stepped casually to the other side. Her next serve, too, was solid. Nicole got a racquet on the ball, but the impact broke the strings and the ball careened away. Nicole took a brief timeout to exchange the racquet for one of Erin's other three. After a practice stroke,

Nicole was once again ready to continue. As Andrea's serve dropped in, Nicole hit it with some backspin, low to Andrea's forehand. Andrea rushed over and returned an under-spin approach shot deep up the line to Nicole's backhand and followed it in. Nicole rushed over, set herself, and took the ball cross-court with her patented backhand. Anticipating, Andrea lunged with a backhand volley, cutting the ball off to the opposite court for a winner. The crowd cheered.

With the score 40-love; Andrea was feeling good and ready for a comeback. One of the next three points would give her the game. Andrea's first serve was long. Her second was good, and Nicole drove it deep to her backhand side. She ran over and missed on her attempt down the line; 40-15. Andrea readied herself, then delivered another big serve and followed it in. Anticipating, Nicole hit the ball to the opposite court to pass her. Again Andrea lunged—this time with a forehand, to send the ball to the open court for a winner. Once again cheers erupted.

"Wow, another perfect volley by Andrea!" called Harper.

Andrea now owned game one. The players switched sides, and then Nicole got ready. Her first serve was good. After several rallies, Andrea attacked Nicole's short ball and sent it to the corner for a winner. On the next point she returned Nicole's serve with a high topspin ball deep on the baseline and approached. Nicole lobbed back, but the ball fell short. Andrea took a step back and hit a powerful overhead for a winner.

Nicole had won all of her service games, but at love-30

she needed to get going very soon. Her next serve missed; Andrea pummeled her second serve right back and followed the ball in. Nicole was forced to offer a weak return that Andrea jumped on top of, volleying the ball softly as a drop shot; love-40.

Nicole needed to respond. She reared back; hit a big serve down the middle—an ace. The crowd cheered. Her next attempt was long. She readied her second, served, and both girls rallied again from the baseline. After a variety of shots, Andrea unleashed a crushing forehand that Nicole couldn't get a racquet on. The crowd yelled.

Andrea had broken Nicole and was now up 2-0. Her demeanor clearly showed her new disposition. Brimming with confidence, she knew how to attack Nicole. Andrea lined up, and served. Again Nicole returned the ball short and Andrea scooped the ball up for another drop-shot winner. Then, in short order, Nicole was unable to return the next two serves; 40-love. Andrea reared back mightily, but the attempt was long. As a surprise, she hit a first serve on her second attempt. Nicole prematurely stepped forward. The serve was good, leaving Nicole watching the ball as it zoomed by; 3-0.

Amid more general comments and murmurs, the girls changed sides. Andrea had taken control of the match. Even Nicole felt it. Andrea had won three games in a row and, even though she lost the first set, led in total games seven to six. If Nicole hoped to survive, she needed an immediate answer.

# 17

**MATCH POINT**

Nicole sat down for a few minutes, then recapped her water jug, before making her way back onto the court. It was her serve—time for a change. A hush descended as Nicole made her toss. The serve was true, but came off Andrea's racquet like a bullet, leaving Nicole with a running backhand along the baseline as Andrea quickly rushed up. Nicole's return sunk at Andrea's feet. Somehow she scooped the ball up gently over the net, to a loud ovation from the crowd; love-15.

Nicole gathered herself. Her serve struck the top of the tape and skipped away. Her second serve, too, hit the net and landed out; double-fault, love-30.

Nicole grew empty inside. She had to keep her game face or Andrea would smell blood. She knew this.

"Andrea has taken control, and with her power and strength, will likely take the set and the match." Mr. Harper concurred.

"And Mia said this would be just like any other match? I have to get it together and play my best. *Now!*" Nicole reminded herself.

Nicole could hear her heart thumping wildly in her chest. She paused and took a few seconds to line up. She recalled Jeff's sage advice. "In the face of change, breathe. Center yourself; calm yourself."

She took a few deep breaths, centered herself, and calmed herself. She glanced up to see Mia, sitting calmly, hands folded. It did wonders to calm Nicole. Now ready, she bounced the ball four times, tossed, and sent a rocket past

Andrea for an ace. The crowd cheered.

Again Nicole lined up, readied herself. Her next serve was almost as good, but Andrea whacked it right over Nicole's head as she ducked. In thirty seconds it was 30-30. Nicole missed her next serve. Andrea drove the second strongly to Nicole's backhand. Nicole ran over the baseline, set her feet as Andrea moved to the net, pointed her right foot and hit a dart that painted the line; 40-30. Nicole's next serve took Andrea completely off the court to her backhand side. Nicole followed the ball in and easily punched the short return to the opposite court. The crowd roared.

The monkey was off Nicole's back. After losing three games in a row, she was finally back on the winning track. With a look of dismay, Andrea stepped up to the service area. She was determined to stop Nicole's surge.

Each held serve for the next four games. Each game was close and demonstrated the best both players had to offer. The crowd couldn't get enough and applauded each and every point.

Harper told the audience, "The best way to describe this match, ladies and gentlemen, is strength versus quickness. The power of Andrea is unbelievable, but Nicole's quickness to the ball and her ability to keep the ball away from Andrea's power positions is—incredible."

Down 3-5, Nicole had not been able to break Andrea's serve this set. If Andrea wins this game, she would take the set. Andrea prepared to serve, uncoiled and hit a rocket. Nicole however, anticipated the ball perfectly, and blasted it back into the open court. The crowd erupted.

The players moved over. Andrea missed her next serve. Nicole drove the second crisply and deeply to her opponent's backhand. Andrea returned the ball across court, but short. Nicole stepped up and drove the ball down the line for a clear winner; love-30. The crowd cheered and shouted approval.

Nicole knew she had a great chance to break Andrea's serve, and dug in. The next offering was a missile, but Nicole once again read it well and responded with a winner; love-40.

Nicole returned the next serve deep down the middle. Andrea drove it to Nicole's right with a powerful forehand, and followed it in. Nicole sprinted across the baseline, jumped off her right foot, and smashed the ball across court—a sinking topspin shot. Andrea, who anticipated a return down the line, stretched her racquet, but the ball was out of reach. The crowd applauded.

"Wow!" said Harper. "This young lady from Milwaukee has pulled another rabbit out of her hat. She's got the poise of a veteran. Andrea just can't seem to close the book on this set."

This game, and especially her last shot, served to re-build Nicole's confidence. Breathing new life into her game, Nicole was only down one game. If she could hold serve, she would tie up the match. The players switched sides, got a quick drink, and walked to their spots. Nicole received the balls, stepped up to the line, bounced the ball exactly four times, and tossed. Her serve was good—and powerfully returned. Quickly Nicole shuffled her feet in preparation to return a powerful forehand to Andrea's backhand side. With time to spare, Andrea set up, and hit a return down the line. Nicole moved to her right and unleashed a huge, cross-court forehand. With time only to hit on the run, Andrea raced across the baseline. Nicole moved in. Andrea took the shot across the court, hoping to pass, but Nicole's two-foot jump stop allowed her to reach back. She dinked the ball to the opposite court for a winner. The crowd cheered.

"Way to go Nic!" Jon yelled.

Nicole lined up, then unleashed a booming serve that Andrea was unable to reach; 30-love. Nicole's next serve was out, but the second was good, and the two faced each other from their baseline. After several hits, Nicole chose an unexpected under-spin forehand short up the line. Andrea could only respond with her own underspin shot back down the same line, as each girl stood at the service line. Andrea's shot caught the net and lifted about five feet from the net on Nicole's side. As Nicole hustled in, Andrea's only chance was to move in a direct line with Nicole's oncoming volley. The return hit Andrea in the hip and bounced off.

"Andrea—are you okay?" Nicole asked.

Andrea glared at Nicole, and stalked away. The crowd murmured.

"The war's going to escalate, folks—I can *feel* it," remarked Harper."

Andrea returned the next serve sharply, near Nicole's

feet. Nicole jumped out of the way, and the umpire signaled out. The score was now tied; 5-5.

"She's fought back from one-four. *Is* she the Comeback Kid?" asked Harper.

As Andrea lined up to serve, the energy was palpable in the stadium. She seemed confident as she set her feet. The murmurs ebbed as her motion began. Gently she tossed the ball, and unleashed a vicious serve. Nicole made contact, but the ball landed in the net.

The ball boy handed Andrea a ball and she lined up again. Aware that she had enjoyed more success from the ad side, Nicole dug in, edging back and forth. Again the serve came, as if shot from a cannon. Nicole gauged, and confidently smacked it back at Andrea, who leapt out of the way. The ball appeared to hit the line. "Good!" the chair umpire signaled.

"What?" shouted Andrea as she frowned at the umpire.

Sternly the umpire called—"Fifteen all."

Fuming, Andrea moved over. Her next serve was long, but her second was a fine effort that Nicole smoked back down the line. The crowd roared; 15-30.

Andrea bit her bottom lip as she served. The ball skimmed the inside line of the service box and zoomed past Nicole—so fast that Nicole didn't see it land. "Thirty-thirty," called the umpire. Nicole nodded and moved over. Andrea served again. Nicole's soft return landed near the baseline. With ample time to prepare, Andrea drove the ball high and deep to Nicole's backhand. Nicole took the ball on the rise and sent it back solidly. Andrea drove the ball up the line, leaving Nicole scurrying in an attempt to retrieve it. As Nicole prepared for the shot, she noticed Andrea edging to the net. At the last second she opened her racquet head and delivered a topspin lob deep to the opposite court. The ball descended, touching the corner. The crowd roared.

Nicole disguised her shot selection so well, it left Andrea with no chance of return; 30-40, break point.

"Up to this point, no one has broken Andrea—Until now! This is all incredible, so unexpected," said Harper.

"Come on Andrea! You can do it!" called a fan. Then the crowd fell into an eerie silence.

Andrea bounced the ball firmly, twice, and tossed. The serve was hard and accurate. Off her two-foot jump stop, Nicole focused on the ball, and caught it crisply on the rise— her racquet hitting the ball only a split second after Andrea. Nicole's return was a dart, but it caught the net. The ball then did a curious thing. It ricocheted two feet up and came down, hitting the net a second time, and fell on Andrea's side; point, game Nicole.

The crowd cheered and whistled. Many stood to show their approval.

"She's broken her again! Four in a row! She *may* be the Comeback Kid!" shouted Harper.

After a short water break, the girls switched sides. They made their way back onto the court amid cheers. The ball boy handed the balls to Nicole.

"Thanks," said Nicole.

As she set herself, the crowd sat down. Again she bounced the ball firmly, four times, and made her toss. Andrea was all over the serve. With a huge swing producing a loud whack, the ball hit inbounds on the opposite side and bounced up against the back wall; love-15.

As the cheers erupted, Nicole lined up. Again Andrea made solid contact—this time to the opposite court for a winner. Amid the roars, Nicole realized, she couldn't squander her serving opportunity. Her next serve was long. As Andrea edged in to attack the spin serve, Nicole decided to try another first serve. She recalled Jeff's words—"If you believe in yourself, *take* risks." Nicole's first-serve percentage had been high for the day, but Andrea's returns had also been outstanding. Nicole lined up, took a deep breath, tossed, and swung solidly through the ball. Andrea had no time to react. Her hand caught in the cookie jar, she barely got a racquet on the ball, and struck it into the net; 15-30.

Nicole exhaled deeply, in relief. Risk had brought its reward. Once again, her first serve was returned deep. She sent the ball back across court, and made her way back to the middle. Both players hit crosscourt backhands back and forth until Andrea went up the line with a penetrating shot. Nicole scurried over, but Andrea's shot was inches too long; 30-30.

Nicole's next serve was in but clipped the net.

"Net serve," called the umpire.

She lined up and delivered the ball, which Andrea returned hard and deep to the backhand. Again Nicole raced across the baseline and, as Andrea moved in for the kill, sent a crisp running backhand off her left foot and down the line. Anticipating this offering, Andrea intercepted the ball with a half-volley to the open court—a winner.

The voices grew louder as the score was now 30-40; break point for Andrea. Nicole lined up, and caught the serve just right. She aced Andrea to the outside of the box. At once the crowd was on its feet, applauding wildly.

"One real nail-bitter, folks!" said Harper.

Nicole's next serve was returned straight up the middle. After three crisp shots apiece, Andrea smoked a forehand.

"Out!" the umpire called.

Andrea paused, looking on in disbelief. In unison the crowd voiced, "Ohhhh!"

Harper chimed in. "Believe it or not, the little lady from Milwaukee is sitting—at match point. Who'd have *thought*?"

Nicole gathered herself to serve. All around her, the crowd was standing.

"One point. Just one more point." Nicole repeated as a mantra.

She set her feet and took a deep breath.

"Please Lord, give me strength!" she murmured. Her toss was perfect, her shot accurate, right in the box. Again Andrea returned the ball deep up the middle. Wanting to keep the ball at Andrea's backhand, Nicole aimed the ball across court but left the shot short. Andrea saw the opening, and delivered with her best backhand of the day, across court, deep to the corner. A scampering Nicole managed an off-balance backhand down the line, then slipped and fell. Andrea ran the ball down and smacked a huge forehand cross court. Up on her feet again, Nicole raced for the open court. Andrea's rocket was already in flight. The ball hit the top of the net, arched and landed two feet over on Nicole's side. Nicole ran, determined. The ball hit the court and bounced up about eighteen inches leaving Nicole with little choice. She dove through the air towards the ball, already on its downward flight, and landed with her racquet fully extended. Somehow she shoved its head under the ball, and flipped her wrist, turning her body from the net as she skidded along the court. The ball landed just over the net. Andrea quickly rushed over, but had no chance of retrieval.

"Good," the umpire signaled.

Nicole, still in a heap, rolled over. All around her people cheered, hooted, and whistled.

With a bloody knee, Nicole got up, reached across the net, and shook Andrea's hand.

"—best shot I have *ever* seen. Move over, Boris Becker!" shouted Harper.

The cheers continued, louder and louder. Back in Milwaukee the nursing staff and Doctor Stanwood broke into celebration. Mr. Novak jumped up and down, hugging his wife. At the club, Jeff turned to the staff. "I *taught* her that shot," he announced. The St. Elizabeth's eighth-grade class erupted into cheers. Sister Clara began dancing with Father Tom.

Nicole looked up, and smiled. Carol, Jon and Mia were clapping loudly. Mr. Nelson and Jim were both grinning and giving her 'a thumbs up.' All the coaches stood and clapped.

After a hearty applause, the tournament director quieted the crowd. She presented Shannon the fourth-place, and Sara the third-place trophy. As she presented Andrea her second-place award, a lengthy round of applause erupted from the crowd. She paused for a moment, and then told the cheering crowd, "In one of the best matches I have *ever* witnessed, I am extremely proud to present the *National Championship trophy* to our fine competitor from Milwaukee, Wisconsin—Nicole Harris!"

The crowd broke into ecstatic cheers, whistles, and shouts. Nicole raised the trophy high over her head. The cheers continued—a standing ovation now. Nicole walked to the edge of the crowd, removed her headband, and handed it to Mr. Henry Nelson. As she handed him the headband, the initials N.H. laid upside down—and now displayed H.N.

"I guess it's never been just mine. It's always been both of ours," Nicole told him.

Nicole looked to Mia, who smiled broadly and said, "I *told* you it would be just like any other match!"

Nicole handed Mia the trophy. "Some sixty years late? Better late than never, Gram!"

Mia propped the trophy atop her head. The crowd cheered.

A reporter edged up. "May I ask you a few questions?"

she inquired.

As Nicole nodded, she posed the question, "Nicole—can you tell our viewers how you are feeling right now?"

"Fantastic. Absolutely, *fantastic!*"

"And about the match—?"

"Andrea Phillips is a great player. I was fortunate—very fortunate—to win today."

"How's your knee? You took a nasty spill on the court."

"A bit sore, but it'll be fine."

"Nicole, would you like to say hello to anyone?"

Nicole nodded, looking into the camera. "Yes. I would like to say hi to the Novaks, the Stanwoods, Jeff and the staff at the Country Club, Carrie, Cindy and all my classmates at St. Elizabeth's—my friend Erin and my Dad."

"Your Dad wasn't able to make it today?"

"No, he was here. The whole match!"

"Nicole, you're a very personable young lady. Have you given any thought to what you'd like to do after a tennis career?"

Nicole reflected. "All I ever wanted to do was play tennis. I love it. It means so much to me." "But if I couldn't play anymore?"

"Hmm, actually what *you* do for a living seems like a great job. It must be very interesting and rewarding!"

"Wow! I think that you would make a great reporter—or, for that matter, anything you'd set your mind to do!" She grinned. "Okay, say you *were* a reporter. What would you ask me?"

Nicole was pensive for a moment then asked, "Do *you* have a real passion for reporting the news?"

"I love reporting the news. Actually, I *am* passionate about finding each story and getting it right!" She nodded. "An excellent question, Nicole!"

The reporter turned directly to the camera. "This is Marie Beyer, Fox Six, your Coastal news leader, with our brand-new national champion *and* newest reporter Nicole Harris signing off from the University of San Diego."

The Smith twins had a solid tournament, finishing second to another set of twins, the Browns from Fresno—they were brunettes!

All things considered, Wisconsin had a fine showing.

## THE END

# Epilogue

Late Monday night the Harrises arrived home. As the car pulled into the driveway, the headlights hit the house, illuminating a huge banner across the front.

## Welcome Home, Champ!

Nicole's entire eighth-grade class had made and signed the banner.

Within a few days Nicole called and thanked everyone for their support and was back into her normal routine. It had been a year of great change for Nicole Harris. However, some things didn't change. Nicole still loved her family, cherished her friends, continued her deep faith in the Lord and her belief in herself. These are the cornerstones of life itself, and make everything and anything possible.

Yes, Mia was right, 'Love Must Mean Something.' Family and friends had always been there for Nicole. Even though her Dad and Erin were not physically present, Nicole was absolutely convinced their memory carried her, in her time of need. Yes, surrounded by love, you can reach levels that some think are unachievable.

A few weeks later Mr. Nelson called Nicole to extend his congratulations. After careful reflection, he came to realize having witnessed firsthand, the difference his financial support had made for Nicole. He thought about all the other talented Nicoles out there, who might also benefit from financial assistance. Although he had already donated a sizeable sum to help underprivileged kids learn tennis, he decided to fund two scholarships at the local club, one in Erin's name and one in Nicole's. He thanked Nicole for opening his eyes; to see the difference he could make to develop young talent. As for Nicole; she had been invited to join an elite traveling squad of top players in the Midwest paid for by the United States Tennis Association.

In late September, Mr. Novak entered his first tournament. He lost his opening match to the top seed—double donuts—but he had one heck of a good time!